Beyond Myth

Beyond Myth

The Genesis Account: How God Artfully
(but Not Scientifically) Created the Heavens and the Earth
and Commissioned Humanity to Rule on His Behalf

The Creation Series, Volume One

WALLACE R. CLAUSEN

WIPF & STOCK · Eugene, Oregon

BEYOND MYTH: THE CREATION SERIES, VOLUME ONE
The Genesis Account: How God Artfully (but Not Scientifically) Created the Heavens and the Earth and Commissioned Humanity to Rule on His Behalf

Copyright © 2025 Wallace R. Clausen. All rights reserved. Except for brief quotations in critical publications or reviews, no part of this book may be reproduced in any manner without prior written permission from the publisher. Write: Permissions, Wipf and Stock Publishers, 199 W. 8th Ave., Suite 3, Eugene, OR 97401.

Wipf & Stock
An Imprint of Wipf and Stock Publishers
199 W. 8th Ave., Suite 3
Eugene, OR 97401

www.wipfandstock.com

PAPERBACK ISBN: 979-8-3852-4971-8
HARDCOVER ISBN: 979-8-3852-4972-5
EBOOK ISBN: 979-8-3852-4973-2

All Scripture quotations in this book, unless otherwise indicated, are from the Holy Bible, New International Version®, NIV®. Copyright ©1973, 1978, 1984, 2011 by Biblica, Inc.® Used by permission. All rights reserved worldwide.

Scripture indicated as ESV is taken from the Holy Bible, English Standard Version. ESV® Text Edition: 2016. Copyright © 2001 by Crossway Bibles, a publishing ministry of Good News Publishers.

Scripture indicated as KJV is taken from the King James Version, published by the National Bible Press, © 1963, a publishing ministry of the National Publishing Company. The KJV is in the public domain.

Scripture indicated as NASB is taken from the New American Standard Bible®, Copyright © 1960, 1971, 1977, 1995, 2020 by The Lockman Foundation. All rights reserved.

Scripture indicated as NET is taken from the New English Translation Bible®. Copyright © 1996–2017 by Biblical Studies Press, L.L.C. http://netbible.com. All rights reserved.

Scripture quotations marked NLT are taken from the Holy Bible, New Living Translation, copyright © 1996, 2004, 2007 by Tyndale House Foundation. Used by permission of Tyndale House Publishers, Inc., Carol Stream, Illinois 60188. All rights reserved.

Scripture indicated as NRSVUE is taken from the New Revised Standard Version Updated Edition. Copyright © 2021 National Council of Churches of Christ in the United States of America. Used by permission. All rights reserved worldwide.

Scripture indicated as REB is taken form the Revised English Bible. Copyright © Cambridge University Press and Oxford University Press, 1989. All rights reserved.

Scripture indicated as RSV is taken from the Revised Standard Version of the Bible, copyright © 1946, 1952, and 1971 the Division of Christian Education of the National Council of the Churches of Christ in the United States of America. Used by permission. All rights reserved.

To Karlen
who, like Eve, is both bearer of life and giver of life,
one through whom God has blessed many,
my primary source of his love.

Contents

Preface: Human Rule | ix
Acknowledgments | xv

Prelude: Six Days | 1

Introduction: | 5
    Section I: Traditions | 5
    Section II: Tools | 19
    Section III: Perspective | 24

    Insert: Enuma Elish, a Creation Myth of Ancient Babylonia | 32

    Section IV: Beginnings | 34

    Insert: Linking the Introduction to Unit 1 | 43

UNIT 1: Creation | 47

    Chapter 1   Creation Under Construction | 49
    Chapter 2   Creation Triad: Days 1 and 4 | 54

    Insert: Gen 1 and the Problematic Use of "Light" | 61

    Chapter 3   Creation Triad: Days 3 and 6 | 67

    Insert: Literary Artistry and Numbers as Ancient Communication | 74

    Chapter 4   Creation Triad: Days 2 and 5 | 77
    Chapter 5   A Cosmic Temple? | 90

Contents

UNIT 2: Garden | 101

    Chapter 6   Structure in the Second Creation Story | 103
    Chapter 7   Symmetry in the Second Creation Story | 111

    Insert: Genre and the Creation Stories | 118

    Chapter 8   Garden Images: "Tree" as Symbol Word | 124
    Chapter 9   Garden Images: "Marriage" and "Serpent" as Symbol Words | 132
    Chapter 10 Into the Garden | 143

Bibliography | 161

Preface: Human Rule

ARGUABLY,[1] THE MOST SIGNIFICANT theme in the Bible is God's sovereignty; that is his kingdom throne.[2] As creator, God reigns over all. That is borne out in the regal phrase "Lord of Lords and King of Kings." Yet, almost paradoxically, the opening chapters of Genesis ascribe rulership of the created order to humanity.

It is surprising, therefore, how little is written in the professional world of biblical scholarship about this theme. Jeremy Treat acknowledges such, stating, "This theme has often been overlooked, but it is crucial to understanding the kingdom of God."[3] Rulership begins in Gen 1 with the creation of humanity in God's image and continues throughout Scripture's presentation of Israel. In that long march toward a future destiny, the race stumbles, falling vastly short of its God-endowed potential to rule well. In the book of Judges, Israel's drift from God is cast under this theme, and so the book ends as it shockingly declares, "In those days Israel had no king; everyone did as they saw fit" (21:25). This leads to the reign of Samuel, the last of the tribal judges who ruled over Israel, a people governed not so much as a nation but a loose confederacy. Ending that way, the book of Judges provides a transition to a coming period in which Israel sought rule under a succession of kings. Yet, Deuteronomy (28:36) warningly records, "The Lord will drive you and the king you set over you to a nation unknown to you or your ancestors. There you will worship other gods, gods of wood and stone." The scrolls referred to as Deuteronomy and Judges point to the danger of human rulership without reliance on God. In the end, Israel's

---

1. Schreiner, *King*, see prologue, xii–xvi.
2. Wright, *How God Became King*, see preface, ix–xvii.
3. The theme Treat refers to is that God "reigns through his image-bearing servant-kings." Treat, *Crucified King*, 42.

experiment with human kings, kings who seldom placed their trust in God, was an abject failure.

This discussion may seem quite distant from the pages of Genesis. Yet, it was in the paradise garden that the failure of the man and the woman to affirm God, electing to follow the beguiling serpent, led to humanity's corruption of the image of God as rulers, be that on the world stage, in the marketplace of commerce, or even within the "smallness" of ordinary life.

Today, the church in America is in the throes of crisis. Like ancient Israel, the church too is falling. It is a divided temple, no longer solely splintered over debates on dogma and norms of faith but fractured by political alliances, much like Israel's kings and priests. The purpose of this book, however, is not to lay out principles of effective rulership or engage in political debate, determining which side is "right" and which is "wrong," or worse, identifying the side "God is on." Rather it is to examine the early chapters of Genesis to (a) develop meaning for the phrase "created in the image of God"; (b) contextually interpret the creation stories; and (c) provide a theological framework to assess the church's current slippage into the abyss of political corruption.

At the outset, therefore, readers must realize that the content of this book is not political; it is theological, even though contemporary events taking place in America provide tempting off-ramps. Taken as such, the story of creation may be read as a plumb line, a measuring stick to determine the church's departure from God's mandate to "rule over" the created order as its falls deeper into the abyss of political idolatry and Christian nationalism.

The danger of this aberration, in which the ecclesia has actively sought political favor, is like Israel's darkened contour in the period following Samuel's rule. In that long period, a time mainly when the nation was split into two kingdoms, threats and assaults occurred from neighboring (and more powerful) nations. First the Northern Kingdom fell, then later the Southern Kingdom. In both instances, the realm's kings sought alliances—not with God so much but with foreign nations who depended on idols and cultic leaders. That tactic was widely condemned by numerous prophets. One was Hosea (13:9–11).

> You are destroyed, Israel,
>   because you are against me, against your helper.
> Where is your king, that he may save you?
> Where are your rulers in all your towns,

Preface: Human Rule

of whom you said,
  'Give me a king and princes'?
So in my anger I gave you a king,
  and in my wrath I took him away.

Yet, this same issue—the desire to solve problems and attain goals by turning to political powers—is playing out again as the church seeks rulers who offer solutions through human agency and alliances. By acceding to political rule, the church's priestly leaders have sought to secure religious aims, hoping through unholy alliances to gain victories they (seemingly) were unable to attain by virtue of dependence and trust in the God they profess. Clearly, the church's alignment with political powers opens it to apostasy, with corresponding judgments and consequences that befell ancient Israel. This, then, is the current context in which this study of human rulership, thematically set in the creation narrative, is established.

This book, which forms the first of a two-volume series, examines Genesis chapters 1–3. In it, the theme of human rulership is taken up. In context with historic Israel, Gen 1–3 may be thought of as the rise of human rule. In book two, however, this theme tragically shifts to the fall of that rule, portrayed in Gen 4–11.

Organizationally, this initial volume is set in two units. The first concentrates on Gen 1; the second finds focus on Gen 2–3. But before that effort is launched, an important introduction gives context and background information to prepare readers to understand the book's content. Augmenting that content, special sidebar "inserts" provide information to consolidate discussions and assist readers in their understanding of coming chapters. To substantiate the book's claims, footnotes and a bibliography are included. To help readers become familiar with cited experts, brief descriptions of scholarly qualifications occur within annotated footnotes. To preserve space, not all referents are listed. This is only a representative sample, a roster that demonstrates diversity of religious experience and wide-scale attainment of scholarship.

One other feature is how numbers are treated. For the most part, numbers follow standard publishing conventions; thus at times they are spelled, while at other times they appear in numerical form. However, to distinguish from normal usages, sometimes numbers are italicized. Hence, the number word "second," or the numerical digit "5," might appear as "*second*" or "*5*." This alteration signals a symbolic or representational meaning.

Preface: Human Rule

In that vein, italicized numbers act like connecting pathways, linking one story element to another. For example, "three" may be used to connect Abraham's *three*-day trek with his son Issac to that of Christ's resurrection as he utters the phrase "and on the *third* day be raised up." Or it might be found in relating the number forty to various scriptural events, such as the flood's rain falling on earth *forty* days and nights to Christ's *forty* days and nights in the wilderness. Sometimes Bible scholars and pulpit preachers use words such as "echo," "reverberation," or "callback" to announce such associations.

Besides these features, a few terms need clarification. Two are "fundamentalists" and "evangelicals." As used in this book, they are best understood in the casual way in which these terms are employed in general conversation. In that context, these words denote both an approach to reading the Bible and its application to life. Generally, then, fundamentalists are those who strongly hold literal interpretations of the Bible and corresponding lifestyles. Viewed on a polar axis, fundamentalists would occupy the farthest reaches of one of that spectrum's end points. Whereas evangelicals would find some adherents along that same far position, a denser placement would be scattered toward the center and even into the other side of the pole's interpretive spread.

Another term, more concept than definition, is "rulership." Often Christians speak of "stewardship" as though a replacement term. While these two words bear similarity, they are not equivalents. Primarily a New Testament/church word, "stewardship" generally connotes the preservation of a trust, be it a skill set, something of value, or even a mentoring relationship. On the other hand, "rulership" is more specific. It bends toward initiative and leadership, conspiring, in a biblical sense, to represent God in taking care of earth's environments in which life dwells. But more importantly, rulership values human life, seen through, for example, acts of justice, mercy, and compassion. Hence, "rulership" is not a political word but is a spiritual-relational concept bound to the phrase "created in the image of God." Biblical rulership brings meaning to all people rather than just a select few. It is certainly not a term reserved exclusively for a nation's kings and queens, its political leaders, but is wide and broad, encompassing all citizens; its definition is forged through inclusiveness and application within the entirety of the human community.

The word "myth" must be also mentioned. There is often great confusion over it, particularly when applied to the Bible. Rather than define "myth" here, it will be developed over the course of this book, beginning with the introduction. Finally, on occasions when referring to biblical authorship, the pronoun "he" is employed. This is done in recognition that Israel's priests and scribes were men and given the common belief that the nation's scrolls were also written by those of that gender.

The task of this creation series is to connect readers to the ancient world of Israel through Gen 1–11's collection of narratives and genealogies. In that effort, ancient context takes center seat, providing the basis for an authentic understanding of the story of creation and the means to look critically at America's contemporary church and its descent into a chaos-filled political environment.[4]

---

4. See Du Mez, *Jesus and John Wayne*, for a detailed chronology of how many in the evangelical world merged into a political orbit.

Acknowledgments

IN COMPOSING THIS WORK, I am indebted to many "voices" without which this book could not have been written. Of those voices, some are listed in the bibliography, while others, though consulted, in the end were not included. For scholarly support, the professional and student library staff at Seattle Pacific University, by permitting access to the college's theology collection during the COVID season, was indispensable. To my manuscript readers prior to publication—my two Keiths—their insights enabled this book to be readable and understandable. Providing extraordinary help was my mentor, Keith Johnson, whose insights, criticisms, suggestions, and above all, encouragements, allowed me to prevail and complete this work. To the editors and staff at Wipf & Stock, with attention to Jordan for his keen insights and helpful suggestions as he steered this book toward completion, the quality of assistance was vital. As was my work with Elisabeth, whose sharp proofreading and skilled copyediting far exceeded my limitations. Similarly, I am thankful for Heather's typesetting competency and communication as she placed this book into its final form. As always, any mistakes in the final text are charged to my account, and for such I apologize for any confusion that might result in the minds of readers. And, finally, to my wife, Karlen, for another long period of understanding and patience. Lastly, to the One Voice over all, the Living Spirit of God, who enabled this work and made possible this understanding of the creation narrative.

Prelude

Six Days

DAY 1. GENESIS 1 verse 3, which announces the onset of light, begins God's creative work. It bridges the description of an earth shrouded in darkness (v. 2) with the commencement of the six-day creation sequence (v. 3). This occurs as God commands the first of "seven Divine fiats,"[1] that is, his spoken word. He says, "Let there be light."[2] That "light" is called "day"; the darkness, which is set off to the side, is labeled "night." This act of separation consumes one day. More so, it suggests to readers whose traditions demand a literal interpretation an answer to the often-asked question, How long is a creation day? Evidence based on the recurring phrase "evening and morning" offers support that a Genesis "day" is twenty-four hours. While not all scholars see it so simply, the context statement "evening and morning" presents a formidable case for this conclusion. Gordon Wenham writes on this idea, "There can be little doubt that here 'day' has its basic sense of a 24-hour period."[3]

Day 2. Verses 6–8 elicit a question regarding the term "firmament." Some Bibles, though, use other words, such as "expanse." *The Message* offers the word "sky." But whichever word is used—firmament, expanse, sky—Elohim (Hebrew generic word for "God") formed it out of a second divine fiat, the separation of the waters above from the waters below. Many consider the waters above to be earth's atmosphere (hence the name "sky"). The second workday is over.

1. Cassuto, *Commentary on Genesis*, 14.
2. Unless otherwise noted, all scriptural quotations are taken from the NIV.
3. Wenham, *Genesis 1–15*, 19. (PhD, University of Cambridge, 1970; holder of significant posts around the world, including at Trinity College, Bristol.)

Prelude

Day 3. Verses 9–13 draw attention to the waters below. God has "gathered" them; this results in the appearance of "dry ground." The gathered waters are called "seas," the dry ground "land." Further, in a burst of activity, Elohim commands the land to produce all sorts of vegetation, plant life capable of replication. All this work God assesses "good," and the third day ends. Unlike the first day's entrance of light, this day, however, with its gathered waters, the emergence of dry land and the addition of plant life covering earth's landscape seems to the modern mind to exceed all expectations for a Genesis-based formula in which a day equals twenty-four hours. This is part of Genesis's mystery: how long is a creation day?

Day 4. Verses 14–19 find Elohim at work in the sky. There he places "lights"; they "separate" the day from the night and serve as signs to mark the passage of seasons and days and years. But their primary purpose is to "give light on the earth." Special attention is given to two lights. Known as "the greater" and "the lesser," they function to "govern" or "rule" the day and the night and to "separate light from darkness." As with the description of "good" on Day 1, so too is this workday labeled. Some scholars see within this day Elohim's creation of time. Still, though, confusion remains over the text's use of "light." Mention, therefore, of light twice—on Day 1 and now on Day 4—adds mystery to the six-day sequence: why did God twice bring "light"?

Day 5. Verses 20–23 recount a heavy day of lifting for Elohim. In one long continuous action he creates aquatics that live in the sea and birds that fill the sky. Seeing that all this is "good," a footnote to the day's work is added: it comes in the form of a blessing. Thus, the biblical writer pairs "life" with "blessing,"[4] thereby associating God's blessing with biological reproduction. The fifth day is completed.

Day 6. Verses 24–31 form creation's high point. It begins as Elohim shifts emphasis to the land and causes it to bring forth animal life. Three broad categories are listed: those that are domestic (livestock), those that are wild, and those that "move along the ground." Following this, the moderator informs readers of a conversation Elohim holds, either with himself or a royal court. We hear God say, "Let us make man in our image." This birthing command includes man's role, which is to "rule over" all of God's good creation and the life it holds. As with the fifth day, Elohim too blesses

---

4. Some creation writers address this as a "theology of blessing." See for example Brueggemann, *Genesis*, 36–38. Towner sees this as "a major motif," one that differs from salvation history. Towner, *Genesis*, 29.

humankind, both male and female, enabling race reproduction. Additionally, God provisions the land's life forms with food, the "every green plant" from the third day. This closes the sixth day, and with it comes completion of "the heavens and the earth." All of God's work is "very good."

The above retell points to a disconnect between Gen 1 and current scientific models. Significantly, that disconnect locates Genesis on the borderline of myth. But many, likely most believers, resist that placement; among them are those who strongly affirm that the Bible cannot be in error—rather it is science which is faulty. Caught in a vortex formed by myth, science, and the veracity of Scripture's creation story are numerous believers. Overwhelmed and bewildered, many simply sidestep this murky debate by clinging to a faith that affirms Genesis's literal depiction of creation, despite a formidable body of empirical evidence. (But in the depths of many hearts uncertainty lodges.)

In this book, the challenge of conflict between myth, science, and the Bible is taken up. Which leads to the question, What relevance can the Genesis creation story, a narrative set some three or more thousand years past, bring to a twenty-first century America rocked by political turmoil and religious fractures? With that context in mind, the introduction lays out a strategy to authentically read, interpret, and find relevance in the biblical account.

Introduction

FOUR SECTIONS COMPRISE THE introduction. The first presents a sweeping summary of how the church has interpreted Scripture over its long history. In the second section, building on that, a question of methods available to the Christian laity—that is, "tools of interpretation"—is asked. Drawing on the church's scholarly world, often referred to as "the academy," three essential instruments are identified. When used effectively, they form an overall reading strategy, one that will be employed throughout this study. Section three concentrates on how ancient culture influenced the Genesis account. That work is followed by a brief insert; it examines the epic poem *Enuma Elish*, an ancient Near Eastern creation myth. Section four concludes by demonstrating the three interpretative tools in a brief survey of Gen 1:1–3.

These four sections—reviewing church interpretation of Genesis over the centuries, identifying significant interpretative tools, building background from the ancient world, and applying these concepts to a reading of Genesis—prepare readers for the task of this book, which is to examine, interpret, and appraise the theological message of Gen 1–3.

SECTION I

Traditions

On December 24, 1968, short segments of the Genesis creation story were read from space. Astronauts Bill Anders, Jim Lovell, and Frank Borman, while orbiting the moon, took turns reading from the King James Bible. An estimated one billion people watched. That reading, on Christmas Eve, was motivated by their desire to address the world's need for peace set against America's involvement in Vietnam. The last to read was Frank Borman; he read from Day 3.

Beyond Myth

And God called the dry land Earth; and the gathering together of the waters called he Seas: and God saw that it was good.

Though the words read by the Apollo 8 crew were first recorded in Israel's deep past, still they speak afresh to human hearts today. For Anders, Lovell, and Borman, those ancient verses offered hope to a war-torn and broken human community, reminding all of God's goodness. To some, however, the setting of the three readers, which was literally "from the heavens above," testified to the story's central character, the divine being known as God. But to others, regard for the crew's setting evoked a controversy over the universe's age when read against the text's literal language.

Such a variety of views brings currency to the debate over what the biblical author meant when he wrote down those ancient words. On one level, the text is crystal-clear. It claims that God created the universe. The astronauts' space-age setting, however, signifies a vast difference between today's scientifically driven culture and those who read and heard Genesis's opening statements several thousand years past. All of which is cause to wonder, What did the biblical author hold in his mind? For him, as his science dictated, the moon was not the same moon Apollo 8 orbited. For him, the moon, which he termed the "lesser light," was one of three objects (sun, moon, stars) set in the "firmament" but not in "space." After all, the ancient writer knew nothing of the cosmos. To him, the daily passage of the sun and the nightly parade of small lights, mere dots high in the sky, were just luminaries—or as Israel's neighboring communities believed, "gods"—casting light upon the earth, markers of seasons and years.

By putting these viewpoints of the "heavens" into a side-by-side comparison—young age versus old age, ancient thinking up against modern knowledge—it is apparent a great difference exists between what the ancient writer thought and how humanity today understands creation. In brief, this is only one illustration of Genesis's many challenges, all of which lead to the primary task of this book: to read and form interpretations out of the narrative's cultural context.

Unfortunately, meaningful discussion of that wide gap is often held hostage by an increasingly polarized religious arena. For many, the tension between what Gen 1 says and how it is interpreted has been turned into a sideshow between conservative "Young Agers" (those who hold a fundamentalist reading of the text) and those who adhere to scientific knowledge, declaring the universe to be of extreme age. This has led to an

Introduction

insistence by some that the age of the earth approximates an order of 6,000 to 10,000 years compared to current scientific knowledge, which finds the universe clocking in at 13.7 billion years. That span is so great that the fudge factor for error alone (some 40 million years) is itself well beyond human comprehension.

Clearly, something is wrong with this picture. But what is it? Is science wrong? Or could the Bible somehow be in error? Or is it something else? Could it be that how we read the text and construct its meaning is the problem? It is at this point that we would do well to hear the words of Kenneth Turner, who draws on his experience as a college teacher in a Christian setting. "Starting with categories that utilize scientific terms like 'creationism' or 'evolution' veers the ensuing discussion in the wrong direction. And once it goes in that direction, it is extremely difficult to bring it back."[5]

Ronald Hendel provides helpful insight. He writes, "It is the narrative style of Genesis—with its mysterious vents, laconic dialogue, and sparse background details—that gives rise to the necessity of interpretation."[6] But to a large segment of Christianity, Genesis contains no mystery. They find within the text an evident "plain sense," a distinct description framed by bold creation declaratives ("and God said"). This posture affirms the text's literal meaning, which is that God created the universe in six days and that those six periods of twenty-four hours occurred no more than ten thousand years past.

Figure 1 illustrates the tension and challenge of reading and constructing meaning for this controversial text. It illustrates how a gap exists between a text's written-down words and an author's intended meaning. The cognitive distance between those actions—reading and acquisition of what an author meant—is mediated by interpretation. This reminds us that as we read, we must determine an author's intent rather than just accept the text's literal language. This is particularly so for Genesis, a book that communicates through a variety of literary genres, all familiar to ancient Israel.

---

5. Turner, "Teaching Genesis," 196.
6. Hendel, *Book of Genesis*, 5. (PhD, Harvard University; Chair of Jewish Studies in Ancient History and Mediterranean Archaeology.)

Figure 1. Interpretation: Mediating Meaning

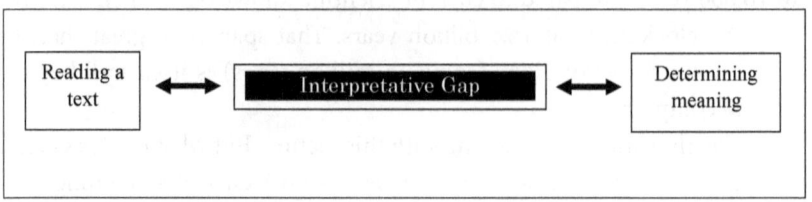

This dichotomy leads to the strange and often mysterious world of biblical interpretation. Generalized and simplified, that world consists of two poles. On one side are those who favor interpreting a text based on its surface-level meaning, which is often referred to as "plain-sense meaning." The other pole represents how understanding rests on the text's richness as inspired literature, which may include allegorical or figurative representations alluded to by Hendel. This is illustrated in figure 2.

Figure 2. Poles of Biblical Interpretation

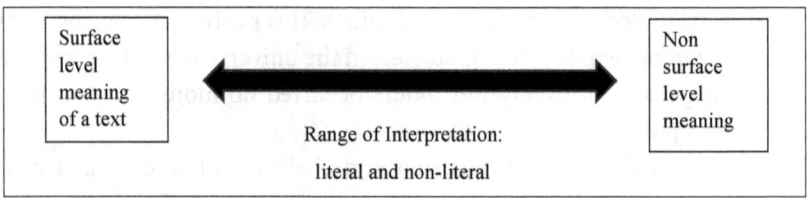

When we read Gen 1–11, at times labeled "primordial history" (meaning to exist from the beginning), we begin by reading the text itself, that is, the inspired words, phrases, and thoughts written by the Bible's ancient author. Without going into a deep discussion on Bible translation issues, what is written is what we read. Doing so places our initial reading on a literal level. But how does such a reading equate to meaning? Writing, reading, and deriving meaning, as functions of communication, are much more complex than a simple transference of literal words yielding literal meanings. Though, in the Christian world today, that is often contested. In part, this is due to uncertainty over biblical inspiration. Many are under the impression that the biblical text, since it is in fact inspired writing, always equates meaning in the same literal way it was constructed. That idea is built on the logic that the text's literal words must be true since God cannot lie.

INTRODUCTION

Church Traditions and Interpretation

For some Bible readers, there resides mainly a single path to textual meaning, and that is through literal interpretation. That pathway is followed by many readers other than when encountering obvious figurative statements, such as poetic passages or parables. On the other hand, non-conservative branches of the church are more likely to read the text by figurative means. This bipolarity of preference has quite literally divided the contemporary church world, affecting both Protestant and Catholic spheres. Such an interpretive gap is the point of figure 2. All of which returns us to Hendel's point: "the necessity of interpretation."

The act of interpretation, though, is guided by at least two considerations. One is what has been termed *hermeneutical principles*. The word "hermeneutics" brings us to one of the goals of this book, which is to narrow the gap between the academic world of professional theologians and lay readers. The second consideration is more personal, sketched out by individual preference. In other words, literal readers construct literal meanings because, at a core level, they believe that's how the Bible should be read. On the other hand, those who see in the text allegories, allusions, and symbolic ideas do so because they too, at a core level, hold such an outlook. The importance of these two considerations—*principles of interpretation and core perspectives*—has largely influenced how the church has read Genesis throughout its history.

Yet, underlying that is a vital question: from which vantage, literal or figurative, has the church read the Bible throughout its long tenure? Many in the conservative world assume, or at least posture, that the literal method is the approach most used and favored over the centuries—and therefore the most authentic. Hendel, however, counters that assumption, writing, "Although modern fundamentalists often think theirs is the authentic old-time religion, its lineage barely goes back a hundred years."[7]

Hermeneutics and Twentieth Century Debates

How important is "hermeneutics" to understanding the Bible? And what does "hermeneutics" mean? Moises Silva offers a streamlined definition. It is "the discipline that deals with principles of interpretation."[8] While Silva

---

7. Hendel, *Book of Genesis*, 194.
8. Silva, *Misread the Bible*, 15. (PhD, University of Manchester; instructor,

agrees that most of the Bible is easy to comprehend, yet for the more difficult parts, and presumably Gen 1–11 is such, a hermeneutical principle is essential. He therefore adds, "The process involved in understanding a text is quite complicated,"[9] after which he elaborates, "when we approach the Bible, however, we see a book written neither in English nor in a modern language closely related to English. Moreover, we are faced with a text that is far removed from us in place and in time."[10]

One cause for such divergent methods of interpretation is how believers regard "inerrancy," which means that the Bible was written without error. While that seems logical and reasonable—that is, the Bible, as God's "word," is free from error—confusion sets in when the text speaks to history. Since much of what is written in the Old Testament is historical in scope, considerable potential for debate exists. Still, for those on the side of literalism there is no room for consideration; after all, if the text is without error, for example the report that creation took place in six days, then unquestionably that is what happened. Or if the text addresses parades of animals and a talking serpent, then animals most certainly paraded, and, yes, a serpent was given voice.

Another factor, "biblical criticism," further muddles this issue. "Biblical criticism," which is a technical term for analyzing Scripture, gained momentum as it swept out of the German academy in the late 1800s. Denis Lamoureux offers a simplified definition: "the careful analysis of Scripture using different methods."[11] Adding further fuel to the fire of biblical interpretation, a few decades later in America, the infamous Scopes Trial[12] blended political aims with biblical beliefs in a courtroom. Based on the recently passed Butler Bill, Tennessee's public-school teachers were prohibited from teaching evolution. Further inflaming the fundamentalist world of the 1960s and '70s was a brutal campaign over inerrancy. Harold Lindsell's book of that era, *The Battle for the Bible*, was written due to concern about the direction Fuller Seminary was taking after Lindsell left the institution. He weaponized fundamentalism as his book became a primary

---

Westminster and Gordon-Conwell Seminaries.)

9. Silva, *Misread the Bible*, 14.

10. Silva, *Misread the Bible*, 19.

11. Lamoureux, *Ancient Science*, 75. (PhD dentistry, University of Alberta; ThD St. Michael's, Toronto; PhD biology, University of Alberta; Professor of Science and Religion, University of Alberta.)

12. Wikipedia. "Scopes Trail." For a contemporary look at scopes, see Swamidass, "Reframing Scopes," 62–66.

Introduction

response from conservatives in defense of an inerrancy-based hermeneutic. One quote illustrates this view: "The battle that rages over the Bible today centers around the question of infallibility—whether the Bible is fully or partially trustworthy."[13]

In many respects, that debate is more deeply fueled today, though its locus-foundation has shifted decidedly toward a venue in which conservatists, both political and religious, have joined hands in a pact aimed at defeating the ills of political liberalism and, on the religious front, the "new hermeneutic." The later term was found in Lindsell's book, near its close, as he wrote, "Today there are evangelicals who, consciously or unconsciously, have drunk deep from the fountains of the *new* hermeneutic."[14] Lindsell, once an editor of *Christianity Today* and a founder of Fuller Seminary, writes, "In our generation an old element that has assumed significant proportions has come to negate the doctrine of biblical infallibility. I refer to the field of biblical interpretation, more popularly thought of under the label 'hermeneutics.'"[15]

One cause for this debate is the false assumption that the Bible has always been faithfully interpreted by literal principles. Here, Lindsell leans toward an interpretation based on a surface-level meaning of words. He states, "It is possible to destroy the idea of biblical infallibility neatly by providing interpretations of Scripture at variance with the plain reading of the texts."[16] This perception holds that all events reported in the Bible took place precisely as described—that is, in accordance with the "plain-sense" meaning of those words—which returns us to the Genesis question: were the events in chapters 1–11—creation, the garden, and east of Eden—real events, and was the history it reports actual history? Conclusively so, Lindsell affirms.

Biblical Interpretation Over the Ages

How we engage interpretation follows mainly from how we look at Scripture. If we hold views like Lindsell's, then the most natural way (and only

---

13. Lindsell, *Battle*, 23. For books written in response to the hermeneutical question, see Conn, *Inerrancy and Hermeneutic*, and Bloesch, *Holy Scripture*, which cover, respectively, the 1980s and 1990s. See Conn for a historical review of this issue in "A Historical Prologue: Inerrancy, Hermeneutic, and Westminster," 15–34.

14. Lindsell, *Battle*, 205.

15. Lindsell, *Battle*, 39.

16. Lindsell, *Battle*, 39.

way) is to read the Bible from a plain-sense lens. And yet, that viewing has not always been held. Joy Schroeder, serving as editor of a book on medieval interpreters (roughly the mid-700s to the Reformation) wrote, "For readers and the church today, critical engagement with medieval exegesis counteracts the twin dangers of amnesia and nostalgia. One temptation is to study the Bible as if its interpretation had no past."[17] Furthermore, Schroeder claims, "Medieval interpreters inherited from the early church the 'fourfold sense' of scripture, the idea that a biblical text may be interpreted in four different senses: literally, allegorically, morally (or tropologically), and anagogically."[18]

James Kugel reports similarly but expresses it differently. "There are essentially four fundamental assumptions about Scripture that characterize all ancient biblical interpretation." The first he lists as "cryptic" texts.[19] Hendel, writing with regard to Kugel, summarizes these as "cryptic, relevant, perfect, and divine."[20] Of cryptic texts he notes, "some[times] the language is obscure or archaic."[21] Essentially, this type of text holds a "deeper cryptic meaning," one not immediately seen though a surface-level reading.[22]

Peter Bouteneff, in a study on how the early church (i.e., the patristic period) approached the Holy Text, concludes, "One feature becomes clear from even a cursory study of this period: we do not find a univocal reading or a single method (which might confound those who would impose a single fixed framework on these narratives)."[23] Joy Schroeder comes to a similar conclusion, addressing twelfth-century commentaries from the medieval period in which "authors took variety of approaches—from strict attention to the literal meaning to the development of highly allegorized interpretations."[24]

---

17. Schroeder, *Book of Genesis*, viii.

18. Schroeder, *Book of Genesis*, 4. (PhD specializing in church history; teacher, Trinity Lutheran and Capital Seminary.)

19. Kugel, *Bible*, 17–18; 23. (PhD; Professor Emeritus, Bar-Ilan University, Israel.)

20. Hendel, *Book of Genesis*, 49.

21. Hendel, *Book of Genesis*, 52.

22. Hendel, *Book of Genesis*, 52–53. On occasion in this book, the word "cryptic" will be employed. When encountering it, Hendel's statement, alluding to a deeper meaning, provides for its definition.

23. Bouteneff, *Beginnings*, x. (PhD, University of Oxford; Professor of Systematic Theology, St. Vladimir's Seminary.)

24. Schroeder, *Book of Genesis*, 23.

Introduction

Statements like these identify a schism between the church's past and today's conservatives. Andrew Louth describes the church's early interpreters as those that read the ancient Jewish scrolls (i.e., the scrolls that were Jesus' Bible) as though they spoke to images and types. This method of reading "is commonly called typology, though this modern term reifies something that was for the Fathers more a habit of thought than a method or doctrine."[25] Louth continues, mentioning of the church in "the East," that its practice was "most commonly, *theoria*, contemplation, looking more deeply into the meaning of Scripture, while the Latin fathers came to use the term for the rhetorical figure that expresses one thing through another: *allegoria*, allegory."[26]

The context of Louth's remarks bears directly on Genesis. Having previously noted a lack of Jewish interest regarding its early chapters, in contrast, the church's early fathers and mothers were able to peel back the hidden layers of that ancient document, exposing them to the light of faith now come in Christ Jesus. And they did this by finding important correspondences, that is, analogies between the now-revealed Christ and the words drawn from Israel's ancient scrolls. This wider lens of interpretation came to be known as figural reading. Hendel defines figural interpretation as "a way of reading in which the biblical text has a second level of meaning . . ."[27] Later, he adds, it "contains truth hidden beneath another truth. It is a two-layered truth, one layer expressed in the sensible words [i.e., the plain sense] and the other in the veiled meanings behind them [i.e., figurative meanings]."[28]

As Scripture transitioned from Judaism into the age of Christianity, an early tradition based on allegory took hold. At times, however, this interpretative approach introduced excesses far beyond reasonableness, as allegories often took control over plain-sense content. An example of extreme overreach can be found in the writings of Pope Innocent III, who lived in the 1200s. He erroneously stated of Genesis's two lights (i.e., 1:16), "The sun is the papal office, from which the imperil majesty derives its light just as the moon does from the sun."[29]

---

25. Louth, *Genesis 1–11*, xlvii–xlviii.
26. Louth, *Genesis 1–11*, xlviii.
27. Hendel, *Book of Genesis*, 60.
28. Hendel, *Book of Genesis*, 111.
29. Hendel, *Book of Genesis*, 123.

Beyond Myth

By the Middle Ages, medieval reading had arisen. And with it came the influence of the Roman Church's monastic approach to life and the Latin text. This period reflected several tensions in Bible-reading. Often it faithfully represented the patristic period (i.e., the early church fathers and mothers) in which some leaned toward allegory, for example Origen, but it also provided the seeds from which historical criticism would grow. Yet, this form of interpretation, which Hendel refers to as "figural," was a dominant method for nearly two thousand years.[30] As the medieval years advanced, there came a rise in commentators. Increasingly this approach relied on a "knowledge of Hebrew, philosophy, and science to correct many mystical interpretations of the Bible."[31] Thus, this period sponsored an advancement toward rationalism and reason, and with it commentators began a more exacting study of the text in its original languages, abandoning, in some cases, the Latin translation (i.e., the Vulgate version used by the Roman Church). Still, the weight of the church remained strong and would continue so until the bloom of the Reformation, set in proximity with Europe's Renaissance.[32]

That trend, along with Rome's pattern of abuses, would eventually open the doorway to Luther's Ninety-Five Theses. And with that, the age of the Reformation was born. What emerged was a turn toward the "plain sense" of the text and away from figural reading. Luther himself proved a pivotal player in this switch. Hendel quotes Luther: "When I was a monk I was a master in the use of allegories."[33] Yet, Hendel found, "as his views changed—as he turned into the champion of the Protestant Reformation—he abandoned allegory."[34] As Luther saw it, "The literal sense does it—in it there's life, comfort, power, instruction and skill."[35]

While the plain sense of the text was powering the Reformation, discoveries in science were simultaneously stirring the Renaissance. Eventually that doorway, built upon empiricism, advanced into the world of biblical theology,[36] and with it came a new methodology known as "bib-

---

30. Hendel, *Book of Genesis*, 61.

31. Ska, "Genesis in the History of Critical Scholarship," 21. (PhD; Professor, Old Testament Pontifical Biblical Institute, Emeritus since 2016.)

32. Ska, "Genesis in the History of Critical Scholarship," 22–23.

33. Hendel, *Book of Genesis*, 121.

34. Hendel, *Book of Genesis*, 121.

35. Hendel, *Book of Genesis*, 121.

36. Hendel, *Book of Genesis*, 166–67.

Introduction

lical criticism,"[37] meaning to look deeply into the formation of Scripture. Jean-Louis Ska described this period as a "return to the original languages, Hebrew, Greek, and Aramaic."[38] Here, the introduction of a printed Bible cannot be dismissed for its impact. Ska wrote, "The study and diffusion of the biblical text, in its original languages and in modern translations, explains the flourishing of commentaries in this period, and prepares the work of Baruch Spinoza."[39] Spinoza promoted a "critical" and reasoned methodology of studying Scripture. As Ska attests, Spinoza advocated that "biblical literature should be read and interpreted the same way as other historical documents."[40]

The aftermath of that movement, known as biblical criticism, proved a key target for Lindsell's work. Despite Lindsell's passion for defending a literal hermeneutic, his position mainly ignored the importance of reading the Bible from a cultural context. Among today's leaders emphasizing cultural studies is John Walton. He stresses the importance of reading Genesis as an ancient document.[41] But by largely ignoring or dismissively regarding the importance of Genesis's cultural context,[42] today's fundamentalists and religious conservatives have fallen, as it were, into one of Alice's many tunnels. A leading proponent of plain-sense reading, Todd Beal exemplifies this attitude. "It does not require a person with a PhD to unlock the key to these chapters [Gen. 1–2] by appealing to ANE [ancient Near East] literature or a special genre or some other special figurative approach."[43]

The Present Era

Decades of fundamentalistic resistance culminated in the tensions of the present era, which advanced Lindsell's cry to battle. However, while Lindsell's purpose was strictly religious, that is, interpretation aimed at Scripture's "plain sense," many of today's evangelicals, in seeking to bolster

---

37. Lamoureux, *Ancient Science*, 75.
38. Ska, "Genesis in the History of Critical Scholarship," 22.
39. Ska, "Genesis in the History of Critical Scholarship," 24.
40. Ska, "Genesis in the History of Critical Scholarship," 26.
41. Walton, *Lost World* series. (PhD, Hebrew Union College–JIR; Professor Emeritus, Wheaton College, specializing in Ancient Near Eastern culture.)
42. Monson, "Role of Context," 309–27.
43. Beal, "Reading Genesis 1–2," 45. (PhD, Catholic University of America, Professor OT and Chair OT Literature and Exegesis, Capital Seminary.)

religious causes, have forged a political alliance with those who hold parallel views on the American Constitution. In the end, a large segment of the Christian nation (identified as evangelicals in America's press and by television journalists) has become inseparable from issues held by "America First" cousins. This has led, in the eyes of some, to a selective brand of militant interpretation, going so far as to alter the very meaning of Jesus' words. Russell Moore describes in *Christianity Today* how some pastors received pushback when explaining the Sermon on the Mount. "That was fine [i.e., "turning the cheek"] for those times, but not in a culture this hostile to Christianity. That doesn't work anymore. For this, we can't be weak; we have to *fight*."[44]

This politicized movement,[45] however, did not occur overnight. It is the product of years and decades of religious frustrations experienced by many evangelicals, and American citizens in general, who hold governmental reductionist ideas. In the political storms that swept through the nation following September 11's Twin Tower crisis, two massive cohorts—one based in conservative Christian values and the other in right-leaning political ideologies—began tightening into a colossal, political/religious alliance in which traditional values based on truth shifted to an "ends justify the means" foundation in which deception is the new norm. To illustrate this condition, polling in the aftermath of the January 6 insurrection showed nearly identical numbers of evangelicals who believed the fraudulent claims of QAnon conspiracy theories as Republicans in general.[46] That finding would have been impossible in the Ronald Reagan years, which blended conservative politics with conservative religious views yet held truth in high regard. More so, broadcasts such as *The 700 Club* under the direction of Pat Robertson, and now under his son Gordon, have for decades politicized viewers, leading them toward Robertson's as well Jerry Falwell's and other conservatives' political ideologies.[47] And then there is Fox News, losers of a near billion-dollar defamation lawsuit[48] over voting machines, which blends some form of Christian thought with American

---

44. Moore, "Losing Our Taste," 34. (Writer, contributor, and currently *Christianity Today*'s editor-in-chief.)

45. For a detailed look at this political and religious movement, see Du Mez, *Jesus and John Wayne*.

46. Robertson, *700 Club*.

47. Wikipedia, "Pat Robertson," paragraph 4 in "Controversies."

48. Durkee, "Dominion Defamation Case."

Introduction

politics. Kristin Kobes Du Mez writes of Fox News, it "didn't frame itself in religious terms, but it more than fit the bill." She adds, "White evangelicals were drawn to the network, and the network, in turn, shaped evangelicalism."[49]

All of this not only surfaces the question of hermeneutics (i.e., principles of biblical interpretation) but points to an increasingly dangerous situation in which a large base of Christianity has fallen into a political ideology which embraces "the knowledge that the ends justify the means."[50] To state this issue simply, the danger of which Harold Lindsell wrote has morphed into a populous, political movement that is no longer centered strictly in religious discourse.[51] In an ironical reversal, the "people of truth" have joined forces with political causes framed upon lies and truth denying tactics.[52] Even as recently as the 2024 presidential election, the myth that President Trump did not lose the 2020 election continued to be held, even though his lawyers and surrogates filed and lost sixty decisions[53] contesting that election in court. Consequently, through such actions as these and others, the term "Christian" and the word "church" have increasingly become synonymous with a political party, as seen in the eyes of secular America. But it is not just secular America which has taken note—the fallout of this political marriage is deeply felt within America's churches. Writing in a religious/political context, authors Sklyer Flowers and Michael Graham claim, "The fracturing of evangelicalism revealed that the historic bonds holding the movement together were less intellectual than they appeared but were rather socioeconomic, political, and cultural."[54]

This contemporary, historical context was examined in a piece in *The Atlantic* by Jonathan Haidt, in which he adapted Gen 11's story of the Tower of Babel, shaping it as a metaphor about life in America:

> It's been clear for quite a while now that red America and blue America are becoming like two different countries claiming the same territory, with two different versions of the Constitution, economics, and American history. But Babel is not a story about tribalism; it's a story about the fragmentation of everything. It's

---

49. Du Mez, *Jesus and John Wayne*, 148.
50. Du Mez, *Jesus and John Wayne*, 3.
51. Du Mez, *Jesus and John Wayne*, 54.
52. Kapur, "Republicans Block Independent Commission."
53. Wikipedia, "Post-Election Lawsuits."
54. Flowers and Graham, "Splintered Generation," 38.

about the shattering of all that had seemed solid, the scattering of people who had been a community. It's a metaphor for what is happening not only *between* red and blue, but within the left and within the right, as well as within universities, companies, professional associations, museums, and even families.[55]

To which we might add, the church.

Applying Haidt's ideas to twenty-first century America, it is clear that the people of God's kingdom have fallen into a void, covered in darkness, shattered and separated, alienated from within. Church members who once worshiped the same God in fellowship now go to different churches that reflect their own political views. The oneness prevalent in local churches has been splintered, chopped up by political tensions that revolve around a cult of personality. Russell Moore writes, "Evangelical Christianity—for good or for ill—has long been tied in the public mind to a celebrity."[56] Critical issues that plague the nation cannot be discussed within church walls, not because Scripture prevents it but because the church has lost its capacity to discuss differences, to be tolerant of one another. Somewhere in this politicization, believers have abandoned what the followers of Christ had at Berea: an ability to apply hermeneutical principles to cull deep truths from Scripture (see Acts 17:10–12) and, most importantly, discuss those divergent views in love.

The ability to dialog over difficult passages, such as we will find in Gen 1–11, rests ultimately not on how well we can agree upon every point of contention but rather on how well we react when differences arise, as they have and will continue to do so. We need to learn again how to read, discuss, and yes, bless one another when others read the text differently than "we" do. The body of Christ is always going to be constituted of diverse peoples having diverse views. At the very least, we need to embrace how to read and how to talk about our theological disagreements. If we can do so, then we can learn to handle disputes about political ideas and consequently learn to live in correspondence with what Jesus held in mind when he taught the "abundant life." Clearly, closing this contentious gap between the two poles

---

55. Haidt, "Past 10 Years," 56. This quote from Haidt is a political metaphor and not a theological assessment of the Tower of Babel story. That critique will follow in book two of this series.

56. Moore, "Mount Zion or Mar-a-Lago," 20–21. Du Mez pushes hard at the celebrity factor in her book, in which she names one celebrity personality after another, symbolized by the hard-charging John Wayne. See Du Mez, *Jesus and John Wayne*.

Introduction

of literal and non-literal reading places unprecedented importance on how believers apply hermeneutical principles to form interpretations.

Our task, therefore, in the coming chapters is to rely on foundational principles of interpretation to examine the creation story as an ancient document. At a core level, what guides this narrative analysis is selection of the hermeneutical principle, *literary and cultural lenses open the Bible's inspired language to meaning.*

SUMMARY

This opening segment of the introduction demonstrates that there has been no single way in which the Bible has been interpreted over its vast lifespan. That essential understanding leads to the vital realization that interpretation has always moved beyond just a literal and plain-sense mode. More so, when biblical adherents stay too close to a particular method, such inflexibility invariably becomes a corrupting force. This was the case in the practice of Jewish legalism as it was in an overzealous figurative reading.

Tragically, the assumed view that the Bible has always been interpreted through a fundamentalist lens remains a danger to the church's missional orientation today. This is further complicated when leading figures, such as leaders of world-famous evangelical organizations or television broadcasters, seek support for religious goals by promoting alliances with political figures—men and women—whose rhetoric, at times filled with bombast and self-glorification, laced with anger and even hate, stands apart from biblical norms of which Paul and other New Testament writers advocated. There is need, therefore, to return to a more embracing view of scriptural interpretation, one that looks deeply into the written word without interference from false voices and those who use "God's Word" to gain "their" (political and religious) ends.

SECTION II

Tools

Interpretation is the foundation for understanding Scripture. It navigates the gap between a biblical author's expressed words and the meaning held in his mind as he wrote. In the professional world of biblical scholarship, theologians use many tools to close that distance. Two are essential: Hebrew grammar and Hebrew vocabulary. Upon that base much scholarly work rests. But when we come to the Christian laity we must ask, What tools correspond to scholarly expertise?

There are few Christian laity who speak or read Hebrew and even fewer with a technical knowledge of its grammar and vocabulary. That being so we must inquire, how might ordinary congregants be guided when deeply examining Old Testament passages? In other words, what tools are at a believer's disposal to offset the advantage of practitioners who have been informed by long years of advanced study?

In this segment an answer to that question is given. Surprisingly, it comes straight out of most believers' educational background. In the United States, nearly all citizens are literate. Since the Bible is an anthology of literary writings, it stands to reason that those who read the Bible possess "literacy tools." This leads to two important concepts. First is to recognize that believers already have experience with interpretative tools. Second, congregants have need to learn to apply them when reading the biblical material.

Ironically, these same literacy tools are commonly used by credentialed scholars! Those tools? *Literary structure* and *author style*. It takes only a few minutes of reading theological journals and books to quickly see that much of the theological world employs these tools of interpretation. That fact will be repeatedly illustrated throughout our examination of this series.

Tool One: Biblical (Literary) Structure

Viewed at the broadest level, the Bible may be outlined as having three parts: *prologue* (i.e., Gen 1–11 as introduction), *storyline* (the bulk of the Old and New Testaments), and *epilogue* (Revelation as the Bible's concluding segment). That configuration is an example of biblical structure on a macro scale. In other words, structure is how writers and editors put together various content parts which form a whole composition. Similarly, most schoolchildren were taught that a piece of writing has three parts: a beginning, a middle, and an ending. When students were taught that, they were instructed in the rudiments of literary structure. Thus, the Bible's three primary structural divisions are its beginning (Gen 1–11), middle section (everything after Gen 12), and ending (Revelation). Indeed, the Bible's division into three parts corresponds to Genesis's structural arrangement

INTRODUCTION

in chapter 1. To illustrate, creation is set in a series of threes. This can be quickly seen as the earth is formed into three parts: sky, land, and sea. Once we take up an analysis of this story, we will find that the creation account largely rests on threefold structures.

As the Jewish community transposed its ancient, oral traditions into writings, referred to as "scrolls," over time those writings were grouped into three collections. Thus, we hear Jesus refer to the Law, the Prophets, and the Writings. Structurally, the "Old Testament," a term the Jewish community does not use,[57] is organized by these headings. Israel's "Law" books are the first five books of the Bible: Genesis through Deuteronomy, at times referred to as the Pentateuch. The remainder of the Jewish Bible is grouped between the collections called the "Prophets" and the "Writings." Biblical scholars point to the differences between how Christianity has organized the Old Testament compared to the Jewish faith.[58]

Noteworthy, therefore, is Jewish reliance on the number three. The book of Genesis is an example. It may be conceptualized as having three divisions:[59] the creation stories of Gen 1–11, the ancestral stories of the three patriarchs (Abraham, Isaac, and Jacob), and a last section, the story of Joseph (Gen 37–50). As we investigate Gen 1–11, we will find how an emphasis on "three" organically forms much of its textual organization. More importantly, we will see how *threefold* patterns directly contribute to story meaning.

All of this and more is why David Dorsey could write, "The third task in studying the structure of an Old Testament book is to consider the relationship of the book's structure to its meaning. The connection between a composition's structure and its message is well know."[60] Importantly, Dorsey's contention is like that of other biblical experts such as J. T. Walsh, who writes, "The 'meaning' of a work of literature is communicated *as much by the structure* of the work as by the surface 'content'" (emphasis added).[61]

---

57. Spina, *Faith*, 1.
58. Dempster, *Dominion and Dynasty*, 51.
59. Fleming, "History and Tradition," 208.
60. Dorsey, *Literary Structure*, 36. (PhD, Dropsie University; Professor at OT School of Theology.)
61. Dorsey, in *Literary Structure*, 36.

Tools Two and Three: Author Style and Ancient Culture

Biblical structure forms boundaries that set one piece of content apart from another. For example, the creation story at the start of Genesis is divided into two parts: the first story (chapter 1) and a second, beginning just into chapter 2. Moreover, as we read through Gen 1–11, we will discover a rotational pattern between narrative stories and genealogical lists. Conversely, *author style* tends to unify, that is, to bring together, what structure separates. But an author's style functions more than just as a compiler of data. It lends interest and drama to the biblical narrative through *an artistic presentation* of content. Often that comes in the form of comparison and contrast. Another way style informs understanding is through genre. To illustrate, Gen 1–11 contains several types of writings (i.e., categories) such as story, genealogy, history, myth, and poetry. The importance of biblical genre is addressed by Tremper Longman III:

> It is crucial in proper interpretation of the Bible to know the genre of a passage one is reading. . . . A genre communicates the intention of the biblical author; it is a code that tells the reader 'how to take' the words of the author. Since inerrancy concerns what God intends to teach in a passage, it becomes critically important to recognize the genre of a text.[62]

Longman's claim becomes apparent once we take up chapter one's creation account. By considering genre, a question is placed in the minds of readers as they must wonder which category of writing best frames the initial creation narrative. Obviously, if we see Gen 1 as science, we must explain its several seemingly contradictions with today's known science. Or if we read it as history, then we must conclude that the author was telling humanity (through Israel) how everything came to be. But if it is read as myth or something else, then a different interpretation unfolds. The question of Gen 1–11's genre, therefore, is among the most critical questions a reader can ask. Denis Lamoureux bluntly states, "Determining the genre *dictates* interpretation."[63] Presumably, that is one reason Charles Halton[64] and Stanley Gundry selected as a title for their debate-styled book, *Genesis: History, Fiction, or Neither?*

---

62. Longman, "What Genesis 1–2 Teaches," 104. (PhD Yale University; Professor of Biblical Studies, Westmont College.)

63. Lamoureux, *Ancient Science*, 162.

64. (PhD, Hebrew Union College; taught OT and Semitic languages.)

Introduction

Once we entertain genre, a door into an author's mind opens. But to enter that passageway we must have some knowledge about the society and culture in which the biblical author lived. Without that, we place interpretation at risk. This idea is expressed by Charles Halton, who wrote, "Every piece of writing is produced within a particular context..."[65] He then offers a jarring suggestion, wondering if today's readers are aware of that ancient context. Halton writes, "Readers will first need to understand the genre of the text and how it worked within the author's cultural environment before they will be able to successfully address the question: 'What does this text mean?'"[66]

By noticing *features of a text*,[67] that is, how the author wrote what he wrote, we become a more culturally informed reader. Obviously, with a book as old as Genesis, any movement toward understanding the background context out of which it emerged will enhance meaning. In addition to literary genre, *features of author style* include the already mentioned comparison/contrast but also stylistic elements such as word choice, use of repetition, and insertion of specialized forms of literature into the text (for example, a line of poetry). Additionally, in the ancient Near East as well as in the writings of Israel, numbers took on meaning well beyond quantitative expectations. Further aspects of author style which are set in a cultural context are the use of vivid word-images and figurative writing.

To sum up this discussion, author style, when placed into an ancient world context, is much more than being about skilled writing. Style introduces subtleties from a culture which often are unknown to present-day readers. Without knowledge of subtleties, we are likely to blunder into blind alleys, failing to comprehend what would have been apparent to an ancient reader. It would be like telling an ancient, "Tomorrow I'm going to *fly* from Babylon to Jerusalem" and then expecting her to understand how you could possibly do that. In her mind, she would likely envision putting on a pair of wings! To put this otherwise, author style is much more than a biblical author's word acumen; significantly, all writing comes from within a cultural context.

To understand what an ancient meant as he or she wrote, we must comprehend intent. To do so, we must have regard for how vastly different ancient Near East cultures were from ours today. John Walton addresses

---

65. Halton and Gundry, *Genesis*, 18.
66. Halton and Gundry, *Genesis*, 18.
67. Longman, "What Genesis 1–2 Teaches," 104.

this issue, writing, "Language assumes a culture, operates in culture, serves culture. Consequently, when we read a text written in another language and addressed to another culture, we must translate the culture as well as the language if we hope to understand the text fully."[68] Kenneth Turner wrote similarly, "This means, for Gen 1, that we must seek to enter the verbal and conceptual world of ancient Israel to find out how they spoke and thought about the interrelationships of deity, humanity, and the rest of creation."[69] In short, if we fail to embrace a writer's historic context, that is, his culture, we fail to comprehend his message and its meaning.

SUMMARY

In this short segment, three interpretive tools—*biblical structure*, *author style*, and the importance of *ancient culture*—were introduced. Two tools, structure and style, are foundational laity tools that correspond to a scholar's knowledge of Hebrew grammar and vocabulary. Importantly, most Americans already possess two of these literary tools, which were derived from a literacy-rich public school education. Yet, there is need when studying the Bible to learn how to use them when forming interpretations. The third tool, ancient culture, requires considerable honing for most congregants. When awareness of ancient culture is paired with literary structure and author style, this toolset effectively enables readers to peel back and expose the Genesis writer's intent and his message.

SECTION III

Perspective

The purpose of the introduction is to promote a reading perspective based on historical context and the tools of literary analysis. There is a need, then, to identify and use this toolset to do the hard work of interpretation. This is due in part to those who find the creation text to be at odds with today's science. Such a dichotomy is recognized by many biblical scholars, who address the importance of "inhabiting" Israel's ancient culture as a partial remedy. In other words, there is a need to know the thinking behind the biblical author as he wrote of creation. By establishing a culturally based

---

68. Walton, *Genesis One*, 7.
69. Turner, "Teaching Genesis 1," 201.

Introduction

reading perspective, access into the worldview of Israel, what its surrounding peoples thought and believed, and how ideas were communicated can be attained. Such a perspective enables today's readers to competently use the tool of ancient culture, which is fundamentally a tool of paradigm shifting. That tool, though, is the most difficult of the three to acquire and apply.

In this section, emphasis is on expanding a reader's understanding of interpretative tools. Regarding literary structure and author style, there is less need for augmentation, since most readers are familiar with them. That, though, is not the case with ancient culture. For that reason, this section directly focuses on developing a cultural framework for interpretation. Following that, a brief *insert* explores the relationship between one of the ancient Near East's best known epic poems, *Enuma Elish*, and Genesis's creation story.

Orientation: Ancient Culture

Some occupations require special eyesight devices. Welders, for example, must have protection from a sight-damaging torch. Others, such as carpenters, require face shields to keep objects from striking eyes. Some people, though, require vision enhancements such as wearing glasses. It is this latter type of enhancement that we are seeking in this section. Understanding Genesis is made easier once a reader grasps its cultural background.[70] In other words, we must "see" Genesis as an ancient writer would have experienced it in his culture.

Our proposition is that until we take up ancient Israel's sight lines, we are like a person with limited vision, one with blurry eyesight. But once we put on "cultural glasses," our vision clears. Grasping the importance of this interpretative feature and perceiving how cultural practices shaped biblical communication is the goal of this section.

Thinking Like the Ancient World

Israel's King David is revered for writing many of the 150 psalms found in the Old Testament. David was a man of great faith yet also a man who, in the experiences of life, ran the full gamut of emotional lows and highs, from wretched situations to glorious faithfulness, from sorrow to exaltation.

---

70. This is not to say that the book of Genesis is limited to solely one culture.

Imagine for a moment if we could call up David from the grave as King Saul once endeavored to do with Samuel. What a rich and meaningful conversation we might have! In such a discussion, though, we might be surprised to learn how David's conceptualization of the world was considerably different than ours. That's because what David *thought* and what we *know* stem from two completely different sciences.

In our imagined conversation with David and other "creation" psalm writers, we might be startled to learn how little they understood of the structural composition of the earth, the sun, and the solar system—indeed, how little they knew of the universe. For example, in Ps 8, David wrote of the "heavens" as the "work of [God's] fingers, the moon and the stars, which you have set in place." Or in Ps 4, writing for the voice of God, David inquires, "How long will you people turn my glory into shame? How long will you love delusions and seek false gods?" (v. 2). Then there is Ps 104, in which the psalmist declares that God "waters the mountains from his upper chambers" (v. 13) and how the sun "knows when to go down" (v. 19). Thus, David's thoughts inform us that his thinking was contextually set upon the ancient world's science and metaphysical world.

When these and other creation psalms speak of what today we call "solar" and "stellar" objects—the sun, moon, and stars—those ancient writers saw them as being "set in place" by God's fingers. Of course, we understand this as poetic expression, a literary way to express awe for Israel's God. Still, that sense of awe is conveyed through an ancient writer's science, which is how Israel thought of creation. In the nation's thinking, the heavens were the uppermost parts of the earth. In those uppermost parts, it was there that God literally hung the sun, moon, and stars, affixing them, as it were, to earth's uppermost atmosphere! If we tried to tell David that the moon was a quarter of a million miles away, he would think us crazy. And to say that the sun was even farther than the moon and of such stupendous size that it would quite literally swallow up both earth and moon as easily as a hippopotamus takes up a watery reed, such a notion would be unbelievable for David. As for the stars—those tiny luminaries which, like the moon, traverse the night sky before the morning sun "comes up"—to say that they were set in "space" would indeed be a bridge too far to cross. After all, David knew nothing of the vast cosmos; he had no way to comprehend a universe that would someday be measured in light years. These well-known and universally accepted twenty-first-century facts David would find incomprehensible. He simply had no knowledge of them. R. W. L. Moberly,

INTRODUCTION

having described the seven-day creation, expresses how the ancient writer would think of it. "Second, this [Genesis] is a picture of the world as the writer knew it . . . [it is] a picture of the world familiar to the writer and his intended audience. As such, it incorporates the writer's understanding of the way the world is . . ."[71]

The way David envisioned his world may be glimpsed in many places in his writings. We observe some of these as he describes the earth's "upper chambers" and how those "chambers" functioned. From an ancient viewpoint, sitting atop the earth's sky was something like a huge holding tank, a reservoir. It was out of that chamber that rain fell, escaping as sky-gods opened huge sluice gates which permitted precipitation in the form of rain or snow to fall to earth below. While David wrote to dismantle belief in the "gods,"[72] nevertheless he wrote within the ancient world's understanding of its science and metaphysics. Thus, in David's conceptualization of the "heavens and the earth," he held no idea of anything beyond the boundaries of our planet. Further, as ancient Israel scanned the horizon, taking in a full 360-degree view and then looking upward, what the people perceived was a bluish sky arching to form a curved peak. In their mindset, the sky was a vast and translucent dome, strong enough to hold a watery reservoir. Moberly puts it this way, referring to the work of the second day, "The next step is to diminish the overwhelming presence of water on earth by removing much of it and holding it back with a kind of barrier (a 'firmament' or 'dome') which God names 'heavens/sky' . . ."[73] In other words, "sky" was a vault. It was home to the gods, which the ancients associated with the stars, the moon, and the sun.

Scholars inform us that in David's time, people conceptualized earth in three parts. First were the heavens, composed of an upper chamber (the rain portal) and a lower region in which birds flew. Below that was a "flat" earth, its surface covered by landforms and a watery environment of lakes, rivers, and oceans. Beneath that was an underworld. Of this three-tiered view of creation, the ancients believed gods dwelt in the heavens and in the underworld. In between those two realms resided mankind, sandwiched as it were between the gods of sky and underworld. Humanity, squeezed in between, was constantly threatened.

---

71. Moberly, *Theology of Genesis*, 47–48.
72. Waltke, *Dance*, 164–65.
73. Moberly, *Theology of Genesis*, 45.

Humans were subservient to the gods. The race feared the gods, who held power and control over what we think of as nature. (Even today the phrase "an act of God" lingers in our thinking, substituting for the harsh reality of natural tragedies.) But to ancient peoples, natural events which we associate with the forces of nature—earthquakes, thunder and lightning storms, hurricanes and the like—were caused by the gods.[74] To appease the gods, who were often hungry, humans brought food,[75] placing meals in temples they believed were the meeting and lodging grounds for when the gods occasionally visited the earth. Failure to provide food or acknowledge their presence was to invite disaster. In agriculturally dependent societies in which seasons alternated between dry and wet, humans depended on the benevolence of the gods, understood through the regulation of seasonal flooding. If the gods withheld rain, or if they released it in torrents, then either the land was too dry for crops or overflowing riverbanks threatened to sweep away those who lived too near. In either case, disaster loomed.

Placing this formulation of ancient culture alongside our own conception, including how David and other psalmists described creation, allows us to appreciate what John Walton wrote: "Though our understanding of ancient culture will always be limited, ancient literature is the key to a proper interpretation of the text [e.g., Genesis], and sufficient amounts of it are available to allow us to make progress in our understanding."[76] Therefore, alluding to David and other psalm writers, creation expressions like these demonstrate how Old Testament readers can fail to access a biblical writer's background when interpreting Genesis. While there may be little danger in wrongly establishing what an author meant when he wrote of a sky-chamber watering earth's surface, that is not the case when we read Gen 1 and Gen 2. Failing to comprehend the author's "science" out of which these chapters are formed has led the church to misread the creation text. That danger? Genesis 1–11 is the foundation on which the entire Bible rests.

Concordism

When the biblical text makes statements that are obviously contradicted by modern science, such as the sun, moon, and stars being attached to the earth's upper atmosphere, that is both perplexing and challenging for those

---

74. Walton, *Genesis One*, 18.
75. Heidel, *Babylonian Genesis*, 9.
76. Walton, *Genesis One*, 20.

Introduction

who read the text from the lens of a plain-sense meaning. For such, this presents the impossible task of defending what is clearly indefensible. That need, to defend Scripture, exists in the minds of some believers because the literal word of God can never be in error (doctrine of inerrancy). To satisfy such apparent conflicts, a way around must be found. Three ways to resolve such issues are common today.

One is to remain strongly committed to the literal text. That was the hermeneutical principle advocated by Harold Lindsell and remains to this day firmly entrenched in the minds of many Christians and most evangelicals. Denis Lamoureux reports that "eighty-seven percent of evangelical (born-again) Christians think that Genesis 1 is a literal account of how God actually created the world."[77] Hardcore advocates of a literal reading do not accept the teachings of science when it conflicts with the Bible. The most devoted of this large group are referred to as "Young Agers," implying that the age of the earth is no more than ten thousand years old.

An alternative to viewing a young age earth is shared by those who may be called "concordists." The word "concord" means to agree. Concordists read and interpret Scripture in ways that permit it and science to concur.[78] The difficulty with this approach, though, is that it requires concordists to reinterpret the words of the Genesis writer in ways that they were never meant to be used. John Walton considers this an attempt to "translate the culture and text" of Genesis into the thinking of today's scientifically inclined population. Walton accurately assesses this approach. "It seeks to give a modern scientific explanation for the details" (in Gen 1).[79]

Yet, there is another way to read the Genesis creation story. That is the one advocated here, which is to recognize that the cognitive environment—which means how an ancient world thought and conceptualized creation—was vastly different than how our present culture understands the formation of the "heavens and the earth." More so, in this viewing, there is no conflict or contradiction possible because the two cultures bear no relationship with one another in matters of science. It is not a case of comparing apples to apples, or even apples to oranges, but more like apples to animals.

Importantly, we must recognize that the Genesis author wrote directly to those in that ancient culture. All other audiences, which would be any in

---

77. Lamoureux, *Ancient Science*, 19.
78. Collins, *Genesis 1–4*, 57.
79. Walton, *Genesis One*, 14–15.

the long history of the church, including the present day, must understand that the text was written not *to* us but *for* us. Hence, if we are to understand the creation text, we must approach it from the lens of the ancient writer. Science, therefore, is not the problem; rather it is how we form our interpretation. If we do so by insisting that what the Genesis author wrote informs our science, then we have fallen into mistake and error.

Summary

To recap, Gen 1–11 presents no challenge to biblical inerrancy since ancient writers wrote of creation from within their culture's knowledge. What an ancient writer knew was not a cause for making the text inspired; rather, it *was the interpretation* brought to the creation text by ancient writers that made it without error. John Walton, in describing how biblical authors wrote about the past, states, "The event [is being used] to communicate their theological message."[80] He continues, "Events are not inspired; interpretations of events are."[81] Unfortunately, we have too often failed to understand the intent of the ancient author because we have failed to read his writing within his own culturally based mindset (i.e., his "cognitive environment"). Denis Lamoureux holds similar ideas, stating, "*We need to read Scripture through ancient eyes and with an ancient mindset.*"[82]

To restate this, if we are to legitimately remedy the challenges and apparent conflicts between the Bible and today's science, resolution first comes by disabusing ourselves of the thought that an ancient culture and its science are at war with our culture and our science. They are not. How our science looks at creation and how the biblical writer looked at it are completely different. It is not twenty-first-century science that is the concern of the Genesis writer; rather, it is his theology. We must pay attention to the ancient writer's culture, in this case his science, and how he communicated biblical truths out of it. Which means that we must, to the best of our ability, enter his mindset, enter his ancient world and its way of perceiving creation if we are to understand his message.

---

80. Walton, Flood, 23.
81. Walton, Flood, 23.
82. Lamoureux, *Ancient Science*, 35.

Introduction

CONCLUSION

Hermeneutical Principles: Keys to Interpretation and Understanding

The above section held one aim: to build perspective about the ancient world and its importance when reading and interpreting Scripture. As we transition from the information above to what shortly follows, namely examination of Genesis's first three verses, we need to be clear how we will go about this task. Here, J. Richard Middleton is helpful.[83] Facing a similar situation, his topic was to explore the meaning of the phrase "*image of God*" rather than "creation." He proposed three guidelines for interpretation. The first was to read "the most immediate literary subunit."[84] In other words, to read the sentence and the immediate context in which the phrase "image of God" was located. Next, he saw the need to widen the biblical context in which it is set: in other words, Gen 1:1—2:3.[85] Since the phrase "image of God" is restricted to solely Gen 1:26-27, for him this meant other similar biblical texts, such as Gen 5:1-3, which uses the words "created" and "likeness," but not in the same way found in Gen 1:26-27.[86] Hence, he explained how other passages, chapters, and books of the Bible may contribute to clarifying and expanding a study's objective. Lastly, Middleton considered audiences outside the Bible, writing that his goal was "to explore the social and historical world behind the text."[87] Such nonbiblical sources can include the works of other scholars, as well as the ancient Near East's production of literature and myths.

Our look into Gen 1–11 proceeds similarly. Steps one and two, the immediate context and its broader biblical context, will be investigated through our proposed hermeneutical principle, *the literary and cultural lenses open the Bible's inspired language to meaning*. Therefore, we will rely on *literary structure* and *author style* to investigate Genesis's opening three verses. As for the third element, embracing ancient culture, we will pick up the region's wider cultural perspective by taking note of what Kenton Sparks has to say. In comparing Egyptian and Babylonian creation accounts to Genesis, he finds "the greater similarity is with the Babylonian

---

83. (PhD, Vrije University, Amsterdam; Professor of Biblical Worldview and Exegesis, Roberts Wesleyan College.)
84. Middleton, *Liberating Image*, 43.
85. Middleton, *Liberating Image*, 43.
86. Middleton, *Liberating Image*, 144.
87. Middleton, *Liberating Image*, 93.

traditions, especially with the creation myth, *Enuma Elish*."[88] As we begin our examination, then, we will start with an insert, reviewing *Enuma Elish* as background to our study of Genesis. Our purpose is to see how some of its ideas and concepts are similar to Genesis's creation story. Importantly, those parallel concepts will open a pathway into the biblical author's mind and his theology.

> ### *Enuma Elish*, a Creation Myth of Ancient Babylonia
>
> In the late nineteenth and the early to middle years of the twentieth century, excavators prowling the ruins of King Ashurbanipal's library at Nineveh (circa 668–630 BCE) found tablets and fragments from an epic tale known as *Enuma Elish*. That title, "which takes its name from the opening words"[89] of that ancient Babylonian myth, means "when above" or "when on high." The *New World Encyclopedia* describes this creation poem.
>
>> This epic is one of the most important sources for understanding the Babylonian worldview, centered on the supremacy of the god Marduk and the creation of humankind as the servants of the gods. One of its primary purposes seems to be the elevation of Marduk, the chief god of Babylon, above other older Mesopotamian deities.[90]
>
> Alexander Heidel, who lived in the first half of the twentieth century, was a Bible scholar and staff member of the University of Chicago's Oriental Institute. Of his translation on *Enuma Elish*, he wrote, referring to it and other epic myths, they "have shown that the Old Testament is not an isolated body of literature but that it has so many parallels in the literature of the nations surrounding Israel . . ."[91] Continuing, he adds, "Again and again the annals of the Assyrian monarchs confirm, elucidate, or supplement the Hebrew chronicles of Judah and Israel, while the creation and flood stories of the Babylonians as well as the Code of Hammurabi abound in striking parallels to the corresponding portions of the Old Testament."[92]
>
> Written in seven tablets, the epic tale of *Enuma Elish* is too long to reproduce here. But, as the *New World Encyclopedia* summarizes, it is a mythic poem of conflict between the gods. As the poem's lengthy battle scenes conclude and the Babylonian god Marduk reigns, the tale shifts to creation

---

88. Sparks, "Genesis 1–11 as Ancient Historiography," 127.
89. Heidel, *Babylonian Genesis*, 1.
90. New World Encyclopedia, "*Enuma Elish*," para. 2.
91. Heidel, *Babylonian Genesis*, v.
92. Heidel, *Babylonian Genesis*, v.

Introduction

mythology. It is that correspondence which draws interest for Genesis chapter 1. Heidel describes the creation activity of Marduk as dividing the defeated and now dead and distended body of the giant, watery goddess Tiamat into halves. From these portions the "universe" was created. Heidel writes, "With one half of her corpse he formed the sky, with the other he fashioned the earth."[93] Following that, we are told how Marduk "resolved to create man and to impose on him the service which the defeated deities had to render"[94] (namely to provide meals for the victorious ranks of gods under Marduk). In other words, the ancient gods "created" humanity to be their servants.

Heidel points to the tale's significance. As he does, readers may glean relationships with Genesis. He writes, "If the creation of the universe were the prime purpose of the epic, much more emphasis should have been placed on this point."[95] He offers a contrary thought, however, that *Enuma Elish* is "a literary monument in honor of Marduk as the champion of the gods and the creator of heaven and earth."[96] Further, "the story of the creation of the universe was added not so much for the sake of giving an account of how all things came into being, but chiefly because it further served to enhance the glory of Marduk and helped to justify his claim to sovereignty over all things visible and invisible."[97]

In this background summary, important parallels with Genesis are discernable. One is the emergence of a supreme "god." The correspondence, then, to Genesis is that of Israel's God; he is supreme overall and over everyone and everything. As creator of the "heavens and the earth," Elohim alone is worthy of honor and worship.

Going a different direction, the two ancient texts—*Enuma Elish* and Genesis—both describe creation by parting. (For a concise review of *Enuma Elish*, see Jon Levenson,[98] as well as Miller and Soden.[99]) Of that formation, both *Enuma Elish* and Genesis drew upon a primordial water source, which is a deep sea or ocean. In Genesis, this is pictured as a wind/spirit hovered above or over the face of the deep. Thus, both creation stories were built upon a preexistent material property, namely a watery earth. However, the earth described in these two texts bears little in common with the earth known today. To those ancient writers, the earth was flat and

---

93. Heidel, *Babylonian Genesis*, 9.
94. Heidel, *Babylonian Genesis*, 9.
95. Heidel, *Babylonian Genesis*, 11.
96. Heidel, *Babylonian Genesis*, 11.
97. Heidel, *Babylonian Genesis*, 11.
98. Levenson, *Persistence of Evil*, 3–5.
99. Miller and Soden, *In the Beginning*, 113–17.

not surrounded by a universe filled with stellar objects. Rather, the sky's luminaries were part of earth's uppermost atmosphere.

As we enter the Genesis story, these parallels often seem like arguments in which the Genesis author is dismantling belief in the region's gods.[100] In that sense, we find the Genesis author sponsoring "*a god*" who creates by his spoken word, one not reliant on mythical combat; who is independent of nature, yet ruler over it;[101] who separates earth's environments to give functions; and one who, most importantly, creates humanity not to be subservient but rather co-joined in a divinely sponsored partnership to care and rule over all that has been created. Heidel ends his study with these words: "These exalted conceptions in the biblical account of creation give it a depth and dignity unparalleled in any cosmogony know to us from Babylonia or Assyria."[102]

To close out this insert, we need to recognize that there is no contest between Charles Darwin and the Genesis author, nor is there a debate over the earth's age; indeed, there is not even a question of old hermeneutics up against new hermeneutics. After all, in the view of the ancient writer, there existed only the heavens above and the sea/land below. If any debate remains over Gen 1:1, it might be how that first verse should be translated. That is, in its traditional and iconic phrasing or, as increasingly modern Bibles are apt to do, by inserting the word "when" into the text. Of that controversy, should "when" be part of Genesis's opening lines, we will briefly consider in the coming and final section of the introduction.

SECTION IV

Beginnings

Traditionally, ten English words express verse 1: "In the beginning God created the heavens and the earth." In Hebrew, however, those ten English words require only seven words. Yet, there is uncertainty surrounding that translation. Increasingly, modern Bibles favor a much longer opening statement. See for example the NRSVUE, which considers verse 1 dependent on verse 2 to complete the author's thought. Hence the translation "When God began to create the heavens and the earth, the earth was complete chaos, and darkness covered the face of the deep, while a wind from God swept over the face of the waters." This issue is based on scholarly debate that asks

---

100. Hamilton, *Book of Genesis*, 105.
101. Habel, *Literary Criticism*, 24.
102. Heidel, *Babylonian Genesis*, 140.

INTRODUCTION

if verse 1 should be considered independent of the next two verses (as in the traditional rendering) or whether it is dependent on verse 2 (and possibly 3). For our purpose, we refer to this as the "when" debate. In the section below, we will briefly encounter this contemporary controversy. To summarize these opposite positions in more detail, see Arnold[103] and Collins.[104]

In this closing segment of the introduction, the first three verses of Genesis are examined. Our objective holds two aims. First is to demonstrate the toolset of *literary structure, author style,* and *ancient culture*. The second is to open our study by focusing on Genesis's beginning statements as if understood by an ancient audience.

Examining Gen 1:1–2 plus Verse 3

Verse 1: *"In the beginning God created the heavens and the earth."*

How often have those words been read and interpreted from the lens of modern science? Nearly always would be the most common response. If we randomly asked a group of people what verse one meant, nearly all would say something equating "created the heavens" to space or the universe. Indeed, that's how most Bible scholars present this verse as well. Certainly, by equating "heavens" to "universe," the text has been extrapolated correctly. But does that understanding grasp the thinking of Genesis's writer?

By drawing a conclusion that is creation-based, readers have obliquely moved to the side of the text's primary thrust. Genesis 1:1 is not so much aimed at *what* God did (create) as to *who* did it. This is shown in figure 3, in which "God" is identified as the subject of verse 1. The ancient writer could have made "created" the subject, that is, his focus, but he didn't. His intent was to bring an astounding and radical thought into the metaphysical and mystical world of the ancients. Creation was done at the hand, or finger, or voice, of the one "god," the God of Israel. Further, as the story goes on, Israel's "god" is the only God. There are no others. Bruce Waltke takes up this theme, noting how Moses gave those gathered at Sinai "this creation story, allowing only one God, Creator of heaven and earth, who alone deserves worship, trust, and obedience."[105] Quickly he affirms, "God's

---

103. Arnold, *Genesis*, 34–35.
104. Collins, *Genesis 1–4*, 50–55.
105. Waltke, *Dance*, 164. (PhD, Dallas Seminary; PhD, Harvard University; Professor Emeritus, Regent College.)

revelation annihilated them [i.e., the myths and gods of the ancient Near East] and revealed to Israel new and true symbols by which to live."[106]

Figure 3. God as Sentence Subject

First Phrase	Second Phrase	Third Phrase
Temporal Preposition	*Subject (of sentence)*	*Predicate (with object)*
In the beginning →	God →	created (the heavens and the earth)

Verse 1 is structurally broken into three grammatical parts. It begins with the temporal clause "in the beginning." This clause directs attention to the sentence's subject, God. After that, we are told what God did, which is the predicate "created." That act, however, is secondary to the statement's theological intent, which identifies *who* did the creating. This is the tipping point of interpretation. By structurally locating "God" in the center of the statement, the author affirms that what he wrote is more about *who* than *what*. He does not say, "In the beginning the heavens and the earth (as though sentence subject) were created by God." He fervently declares that Elohim (statement subject) created. Hence, he proclaims, "In the beginning God . . ." Gordon Wenham nicely summarizes this: "The first subject of Genesis and the Bible is God."[107]

As for the meaning of what God created, namely the heavens and the earth, enough was said prior to demonstrate what the Genesis writer conceptually thought. But there is another culturally driven concept in need of our attention. And that comes from within the subtle mode of ancient communication itself: namely, how numbers often influenced a text's meaning. While it may seem strange to modern readers that numbers could play a role in communication beyond digital representation, in the culture of the ancient Near East numbers held meaning beyond face value. Simply stated, they affected a text much like a cipher. Therefore, by favoring the iconic seven-word Hebrew translation for Gen 1:1 rather than how modern Bibles often incorporate "when," the traditional English phrasing directly reflects the ancient world, as explained below.

---

106. Waltke, *Dance*, 165.
107. Wenham, *Genesis 1–15*, 14.

Introduction

In the ancient world of Genesis, the number *seven*[108] signaled *sacredness*. To illustrate, *Enuma Elish* was written on *seven* tablets; thus its very construction conveyed to its audience a degree of sacredness. Similarly, so too does Genesis, opening as it does in *seven* Hebrew words. To an ancient reading or hearing verse 1 in Hebrew, he or she would culturally key into the author's stylistic employment of *seven* words. Hearers would know without even consciously thinking that this opening statement heralds the realm of the gods, or God; that this is a sacred message. Within that viewpoint, the Genesis author is signaling just how radical is this proclamation, with its announcement of only one God. Later, we will return to the use of seven and other numbers to examine more closely this phenomenon of number meaning and textual augmentation.

But for now, we close this review of number meaning by recalling Umberto Cassuto.[109] Cassuto argued that the opening "chapter"[110] of Genesis was built around the number seven. Having noted that verse 1 begins with seven words in Hebrew, he postulated that chapter[111] 1 was structured by seven chunks of thought, with each chunk separated from another through the author's depiction of creation over seven days. But Cassuto's fame in this instance was not built upon the obvious—the seven-day story—rather it came by discerning the biblical author's stylistic and saturating use of *seven* throughout the chapter. He noted, for example, how verse 2 was composed of fourteen (Hebrew) words, thus two sets of seven. Jon Levenson, crediting and echoing Cassuto's observations, points to how the word "God" ranges throughout the chapter thirty-five times, yielding five sets of seven, or how the geographically significant term "earth" was written twenty-one times, thus three sets of seven. The assessment word "good" is found seven times, and to quote Levenson, "The paragraph devoted to the seventh day consists of thirty-five words, twenty-one of which form three sentences of seven words..."[112]

---

108. Italicizing the word number seven informs readers that the number being cited holds representational or symbolic meaning. See discussion in preface.

109. (Known as Moshe David Cassuto, Italian historian, rabbi, scholar of the Hebrew Bible and Ugaritic literature, held positions at U. of Florence, U. Rome; taught at U. of Jerusalem.)

110. Cassuto, *Commentary on Genesis*, 13–15.

111. In Genesis, as with other ancient texts, there were no "chapter" breaks; the text just continued without interruption.

112. Levenson, *Persistence of Evil*, 67.

Applied to today's modern controversy of whether "when" should be part of the opening verse's phrasing, it seems inconceivable that the Genesis author would craft the first chapter with such remarkable attention to the number seven yet not begin the creation account with anything other than seven words! This is particularly so given the meaning that *seven* held for the ancient world. This insight makes a profoundly powerful argument when discussing the question whether "when" should be inserted into the opening lines of Genesis or not. Consequently, we adopt the traditional seven words when citing verse 1 throughout this work.[113]

Verse 2: *"Now the earth was formless and empty, darkness was over the surface of the deep, and the Spirit of God was hovering over the waters."*

FIGURE 4. THREE WORD-IMAGES OF VERSE 2

Description A	Description B	Description C
Formless and Empty	Darkness over the Deep	Spirit Hovering

What immediately comes to mind upon hearing this verse is a word-picture, an image resulting from the author's deliberate use of artistic style. In other words, it demonstrates the author's desire to place before readers a stunning visual picture, one which is immersed in darkness. This is caught through word choice, in this case the Hebrew twins *tohu* and *bohu*, or in English, per the NIV, "formless and empty." In addition to the NIV, there are various other ways of translating this word couplet, for example "formless and desolate emptiness" (NASB), "without shape and empty" (NET), and "earth was complete chaos" (NRSVUE); all express the Hebrew *tohu bohu*. Overall, these two Hebrew words suggest various concepts, such as

---

113. W. Sibley Towner provides a brief looks at the controversy over Genesis's opening three verses. See Towner, *Genesis*, 15–16.

a desert wasteland;[114] an empty, unformed and unproductive land;[115] and a wasteland like a trackless desert.[116] These word-images, when combined, bring clarity to what *tohu bohu* means.

Looking more closely at this verse, as displayed in figure 4, it is formed in three parts. To wit, (1) formless and empty, (2) darkness over the surface, and (3) a hovering apparition, the wind/spirit sent from God (i.e., the NIV's "Spirit of God"). Figure 4 illustrates this triadic composition. The composite image of verse 2, then, is darkness.

Description A depicts the earth sketched without environmental support to sustain life. It is presented as flat, empty—*tohu bohu*—of form and purpose. Alexander Heidel found certain correspondences between Genesis, *tohu bohu*, and *Enuma Elish*. Among them, Heidel described how the Babylonian creation poem opened with "a brief reference to the time when nothing except the divine parents, Apsu and Tiamat, and their son Mummu existed."[117] These three characters were, in the Babylonian epic, water-gods. *Enuma Elish*, as does Genesis, describes a time when only the primordial waters existed (Description B in figure 4). Hence, *Enuma Elish*'s three gods evoked the image of water (one salt water, another sweet water, while the son was a mist). They "were mingled in one, forming an immense, undefined mass in which were contained all the elements of which afterward the universe was made."[118]

Description B addresses the surface of the unformed earth; it is covered in a watery darkness—no land is yet visible. Without light, no life can be sustained; without land, neither humans nor animals can exist. Description C, however, provides the first ray of hope for the unformed and darkened earth. The Spirit of God is described as moving about, positioned above not the deep ocean waters but "the surface [i.e., "face" or top layer] of the water" (NET). This last phrase is a transitional statement. It links verse 3, the coming of light, to verse 2's aspiration of the hovering Spirit. This distinction, the activity of the surveying "wind/spirit"—that is, the Spirit of God—needs clarifying. To do so, we draw upon the NET. It reads:

---

114. Hamilton, *Book of Genesis, 1–17*, 108.
115. Arnold, *Genesis*, 37.
116. Wenham, *Genesis 1–15*, 15.
117. Heidel, *Babylonian Genesis*, 3.
118. Heidel, *Babylonian Genesis*, 3.

> Now the earth was without shape and empty, and darkness was over the surface of *the watery deep*, but the Spirit of God was moving over the *surface of the water* (emphasis added).

The NET, in contrast to the NIV, refers to water twice, hence "surface of the watery deep" and "surface of the water." In a translator note, the NET explains that the Hebrew word *tyhom* refers "to the watery deep, the salty ocean—especially the primeval ocean that surrounds and underlies the earth."[119] In contrast is the phrase "the surface of the water." In a study note, the NET asserts a change from the term for the watery deep to the general word for water. Attention, therefore, is drawn to the "surface of the water" being the "face," or top level, of the "deep."[120] It is this top level "face" over which the Spirit of God is viewed as hovering. But we must remember that this layer is no longer considered part of the "deep," that is, the subterranean ocean of antiquity, which is viewed as primordial.[121] Rather, the top layer is depicted as "water," not "ocean depths." We must wonder, then, about this differentiation, which drives us into ancient culture.

The ancient creation myth *Enuma Elish* begins with three gods, Apsu and Tiamat, and their son, Mumu. Tablet 1 reads:

> When above the heaven had not (yet) been named,
> (And) below the earth had not (yet) been called by a name,
> (When) Apsu primeval, their begetter,
> Mummu, (and) Tiamat, she who gave birth to them all,
> (Still) mingled their waters together,[122]

It appears, then, that the Genesis writer picked up on that watery image which was common throughout most of the ancient Near East. Further, in depicting the hovering activity of the "wind/spirit" (i.e., the Spirit of God) above the top layer—it is the "sweet water" level that the creation activity of Day 2 addresses, namely, the creation of the "firmament." Its significance to the creation text will be considered later in the next unit. For now, what we note is the position and activity of the Spirit of God. He may be likened to

---

119. NET, note 'i,' Gen 1.

120. NET, note 'm,' Gen 1.

121. Brueggemann, writing on a comparison of verses 1 and 2, states, "Verse 1 suggests God began with nothing [i.e., *creation ex nihilo*]. Verse 2 makes clear there was an existing chaos [i.e., the waters coving the earth]." See Brueggemann, *Genesis*, 29.

122. This translation is from Heidel, *Babylonian Genesis*, 18. Note: diacritical marks not included.

INTRODUCTION

an advancing guard, and by means of surveying "the darkness," preparation is made for Day 1's commencement of "the light."[123]

Overall, then, comprehension of the second verse rests upon all three of our interpretative tools. In *author style* we have a stunning image of a dark, blank, and formless earth in which no land surface is present, nor is there atmosphere. The earth is completely void of all necessary environmental conditions to support life. But in the *cultural shaping* of the text, which was not written with our science in mind, the statement acquires meaning through ancient beliefs. Of these, the cultural world of the ancient Near East held that the primary two gods—sweet water and salt water—suppressed the land which lay beneath the "face" of the water. This structured word-picture, composed of *three* phrases, reveals the author's thinking. From the Genesis writer's point of view, the earth was without function; it was dead to its intended purpose, held captive by the all-covering waters of the deep.[124]

Verse 3: *"And God said, 'Let there be light,' and there was light."*

Verse 3 provides an answer to the question of what God will do to shape the earth into a life-sustaining environment. It comes as we hear, significantly for the first time in Scripture, *God speak*. He is heard to say, *"Let there be light."*

Yet, there is debate among Bible scholars as to what constitutes verse 3's "light." This controversy rests upon the "light's" source. For now, we will postpone that debate in favor of seeing how this "light" resolves the plot question of verse 2, which is, What will God do about an earth that is void of life and functionality?

That answer comes as the six-day creation sequence begins. In God's proclamation "let there be light," it is apparent that a deliberate contrast to "the darkness" is the author's intent. This is not a science-based statement.[125] It is a theological proposition aimed at a darkened world inhabited by peoples who surround an "enlightened" Israel.[126] In this creation text,

---

123. Towner writes, "The picture in verse 2 . . . is a picture of a divine observer preparing to do a create act." See Towner, *Genesis*, 17.

124. This reading of the text is in alignment with many scholars who reject, in Gen 1, the traditional teaching of creation *ex nihilo*. However, in a canonical reading, there are other scriptures that (re)install this doctrine. See Towner, *Genesis*, 15–16.

125. Towner writes of Gen 1, "It is not a scientific treatise." See Towner, *Genesis*, 14.

126. Brueggemann, who likely sets this text in Israel's period known as the exile, writes, "It served as a refutation of Babylonian theological claims." See Brueggemann,

God engages in the Near Eastern custom of naming things. In the region's cultural practices, to name something was to claim ownership or control over it. In that naming the writer presses his theological intent. God is associated with "the light" he brings; he is in full control of "the darkness" (which God named "night"). In other words, God is superior to all the gods of the ancient world, particularly the water-gods of the deep.

This is a radical worldview that the Genesis author is advancing in his opening statement. His writing is not concerned with creation science. Rather, his is a sharply focused polemic, a written argument striking down the superstitions of the ancients' metaphysically conceived world while at the same time offering a new vision, a new "god," Israel's Yahweh. Hence, these three opening verses form a literary and theological preface to the creation story.

SUMMARY

In section IV of the introduction, two aims were held. One was to expand understanding of the interpretive tool of cultural reading, setting verses 1–3 under the lens of antiquity and not the telescope of modern astronomy. The other was to demonstrate the combined use of all three tools. In that effort we came to read these three opening verses not as a literal declarative of the process of creation. Nor were they read as an accommodation to gain a solution for how today's science contradicts the biblical account. Rather, we read the text with regard to ancient Israel, that is, the people to whom Genesis was written.

We saw within the text's literary artistry how the biblical author wrote an argument to take down the mythology of the ancient word. By intentionally beginning Genesis with *seven* words, the author shook the foundation of that ancient world, which ascribed belief to a pantheon of "gods." His words dismissed that falsehood much as light extinguishes darkness. The Genesis text, by opening the creation account in *seven* words and subsequently saturating the narrative with that same number, elevated the Israelite creation proclamation when compared to other creation myths, especially *Enuma Elish* with its *seven* tablets. This, then, is a not-so-subtle, in-your-face challenge to those who held a mystical worldview of the "gods." More so, it is a strong declarative to Israel; it is a *prima facie* case for Israel's creation faith.

Genesis, 25.

Introduction

The plot of the Genesis narrative centers, therefore, on the question of how God, as Creator, will transform a water-covered and darkened surface into a life-sustaining environment. But even more important is the thought, What is the theological intent behind this storyline? That thrust will guide our reading as we exit the introduction and enter Gen 1. As we journey forward, we will do so armed with three interpretative tools: literary structure, author style, and ancient culture. These tools will advance our understanding of how the biblical author structured, wrote, and framed the creation message.

Linking the Introduction to Unit 1

This insert draws out essential ideas from the introduction. Its focus is on three topics: the organic nature of Scripture; understanding the creation account; and Genesis's ancient reading audience. This grouping links the book's introduction to the creation analysis that immediately follows.

The Nature of Scripture

When questioned about what the Bible is, believers often look to a familiar refrain, namely, "the Word of God." That frequently cited declaration, however, does not describe what constitutes Scripture as text. Rather, it defines Scripture's purpose, being to convey God's thoughts and precepts for living. How those thoughts are communicated leads directly to the question of Scripture's organic nature, which occurs in a literary framework through its anthology of writings.

Significantly, that form of communication is not science nor, strictly speaking, history; rather its content is religion. In other words, the Bible is formulated as written-down theological thoughts. Here, we need to recall that Scripture's opening stories were shaped by Israel's memories which were drawn upon the overarching culture of the ancient Near East. When the literary language of Genesis is examined, as we will do in this book, we will find that it frequently employs "figures of communication" to express meaning. For example, in the text we will encounter metaphor, symbolism, and representation. Such literary elements, however, are often ignored by those who seek to understand Genesis by reliance on its literal language. In other words, what the text appears to indicate through a plain-sense reading is, in many instances, plainly inaccurate when subjected to a literary filter of interpretation.

Despite a fundamentalist tradition of literalism, there is a growing movement among conservative believers to interpret the creation story through the Bible's literary composition rather than solely its literal statements. Theologians Miller and Soden are two of many who no longer read Genesis strictly literally. Grounded by their personal experiences,[127] they describe Genesis as "replete with figurative language."[128] The importance of that phrase is realized as they write, "Recognizing and correctly interpreting figurative and observational language is relevant to our understanding of Genesis 1 and the account of creation."[129]

Understanding Genesis and the Creation Account

Clearly, then, embracing Genesis's figurative formation is prerequisite to understanding the creation story. Rather than reading it as though its literal wording depicts "creation science," believers are increasingly finding within the text's figurative expression a more authentic way to comprehend what the Genesis author meant. Doing so shifts meaning from a literal and plain-sense view to its organic composition, which is filled with figurative expression and packaged in a cultural context that is several thousand years old.

It is at this point that the interpretative toolset mentioned in the introduction can be applied. In chapter 1, we begin our work by examining biblical structure. This is complemented in chapters 2 and 3 through the author's written style, a style that often draws upon figurative language. Combined with these tools is the text's ancient and culturally imposed background.

The Original Audience

Turning again to Miller and Soden, they point to Genesis's first audience. "The Bible is God's word to us, but it wasn't given directly to us—it was written to other people in other languages in other times."[130] This leads to their question, "What did the human author . . . intend for his original audience to understand when they read this passage?"[131] Once that inquiry is asked, readers take the important step of suspending modern knowledge, replacing it instead with questions of what ancient humanity thought, knew, and believed. Such a reading perspective brings us to the third tool,

---

127. Miller and Soden, *In the Beginning*, 17 *(Miller)* and 21 *(Soden)*.
128. Miller and Soden, *In the Beginning*, 41.
129. Miller and Soden, *In the Beginning*, 43.
130. Miller and Soden, *In the Beginning*, 34.
131. Miller and Soden, *In the Beginning*, 35.

Introduction

which is to read creation from the mindset of the Genesis author and the ancient audience to whom he wrote.

To read creation authentically, therefore, it is necessary that it be read from the viewpoint of the ancient world, the world to whom Scripture was written. By relying on three interpretative tools—*structure*, *style*, and *culture*—the capacity to not only read Genesis as those in ancient Israel did but to comprehend the story as though we were part of that original audience comes into play.

The highest heavens belong to the Lord,
but the earth he has given to mankind.

(Ps 115:16)

UNIT 1
Creation

UNIT OVERVIEW

AS PREVIOUSLY READ, THE prelude summarized God's creation actions as reported in Gen 1. Yet, within that vertically organized telling, which proceeded chronologically from one day to the next, a more subtle and elegant way to read the creation story may be found. That way is discovered by grouping the six days of creation into two panels of thought in which the first three days form into one cluster. That gives rise to a second panel, Days 4–6.

For many, the literary grouping of creation's six days into two panels is unknown. In this book, however, we will begin our analysis by following that framework. Therefore, the next three chapters are based on this triadic construction of two panels. More so, by connecting the three pairs of days (1–4, 2–5, and 3–6), the often-neglected but vitally important theme of human rulership is taken up. The final chapter in this unit focuses on what God was making through this two-panel story.

We will discover that the creation narrative is formed out of ancient Israel's traditions; from that, two concepts are learned. First, creation is intimately tied to the nation of Israel. Like Israel, which too had beginnings in a deep past, a parallel is discovered between the nation's conception as a faith community and God's work to birth earth as a habitat for humanity. Second, with that perspective in place, an answer to what God made comes into view. Our finding is that God was at work preparing earth as a sacred site, one suitable for his earthly temple. In other words, the creation story describes earth being transformed into a sacred meeting place in which its chief life form, humanity, comes to meet heaven's majestic God.

CHAPTER 1

Creation Under Construction

GENESIS AS PROLOGUE

THERE ARE AT LEAST three ways that Genesis can be read as a prologue. Figure 5 identifies those ways.

FIGURE 5. PROLOGUE IN GEN 1–11

Term	Textual Range	Functions As
Prologue (Preface)[1]	Gen 1:1–2	Background for Gen 1 (the creation account)
Prologue	Gen 1:1–2:3	Background for Gen 2–11 (the period of antiquity)
Prologue	Gen 1–11	Background for chapters 12–50, the Pentateuch, the Old Testament, and the New Testament.

As figure 5 indicates, there are three ways Genesis functions as a biblical prologue. These three ways may be likened to an accordion as it expands and contracts. In the prologue's most compressed form, which is two verses, it introduces Genesis chapter 1. A second consideration comes with expansion to mid-range size, which is Gen 1 and the first three verses from chapter 2. This reading introduces Genesis's story of antiquity told in chapters 2–11. Lastly, expanded to maximum size, which is all of chapters 1–11, contextualizing background is provided to read the entire Bible, including

---

1. At times the term "preface" is used to distinguish this smaller scale from the two larger depictions of prologue.

Christianity's New Testament. Thus, "prologue" as used here is an introduction; it provides narrative groundwork for reading Scripture. Without this special literary feature, a gap in understanding the overall biblical drama would impede comprehension.

SYMMETRICAL STRUCTURE

In the story retell described in the prelude at the start of this book, the six days of creation were presented vertically. That is, creation proceeded from one day to another until the six-day sequence was completed. This is the most common way chapter 1 is read. Many, if not most, scholars build their commentaries and remarks around this orderly, stately progression. C. John Collins calls this structure "straightforward."[2] Umberto Cassuto notes that it "is based on a system of numerical harmony."[3] That balance, however, may be further refined by viewing the text's structure as *symmetrically* formed. In that construction, the first three days and the last three form two panels describing God's action over six days. Figure 6 pictures Gen 1 being comprised of two panels of creative activity.

FIGURE 6. CREATION'S TWO PANELS, SYMMETRICAL STRUCTURE

Panel A: Days 1–3 Preliminary Preparation	Panel B: Days 4–6 Completed Composition
Light appears	Occupied by stars, sun, moon
Firmament separation: sky and sea	Occupied by birds and aquatic life
Dry land appears; vegetation sprouts	Occupied by land animals and humanity; provisioning of food

J. Richard Middleton addresses this concept, also using the word "panels." Writing under a section headed "God as Artisan," he states, "Since at least the eighteenth century, biblical scholars have noted that God's creative days are divided into two triads or panels of three days each."[4] John Walton

---

2. Collins, *Genesis 1–4*, 71. (PhD, University of Liverpool; Professor of OT and OT Chair for the ESV of the Bible.)

3. Cassuto, *Commentary on Genesis*, 12.

4. Middleton, *Liberating Image*, 74.

considers the activity in Panel A—the first three days—as one in which God establishes functions. He summarizes, "These three great functions—time, weather, and food—are the foundations of life."[5] In other words, the first panel is preparatory; its work is a prerequisite for the culminating activity of the ensuing panel, the birthing of life. Thus, the first panel announces light (Day 1), differentiates atmosphere from the all-covering "seas" (Day 2), and, after calling forth "day ground," carpets the land in vegetation's greenery (Day 3).

In the second panel, the *preparatory work* of the first panel finds fulfillment. The acts of fulfillment establish, therefore, a relationship between Days 1 and 4, Days 2 and 5, and Days 3 and 6. This is depicted in figure 7, which reads *across* but not *down* the days.

FIGURE 7. TRIADIC STRUCTURE IN CREATION'S SIX DAYS

Panel A: Days 1–3	Panel B: Days 4–6
Day 1: God invokes presence of light	Day 4: God "made" two lights (sun & moon)
Day 2: God "made" the sky vault, separating waters above and below	Day 5: God "created" sea life (the great sea monsters) and atmospheric life (birds)
Day 3: Land produces vegetation	Day 6: God "made" animal life and "created" mankind, all sustained by the land's vegetation
Overall Task	Overall Task
Transforming an already created, but purposeless sea into three biospheres.	Populating the newly minted biospheres with compatible life forms.

In this depiction, we find that Day 4 completes Day 1 with its placement in the sky of solar and stellar objects: sun, moon, and stars. Day 2 corresponds to Day 5, as God fills the watery environment with teeming fish and the sky with countless flying birds. Following that, the author concludes with Days 3 and 6 as Elohim attends to the "dry ground," populating it with animal life—humankind being the last and therefore creation's crown jewel. This overview of creation finds an obvious literary intent, one set on a symmetrical pattern of three paired days.

C. John Collins, as others do, labels this triadic pattern "the literary framework scheme of interpretation."[6] Of this view, he writes, the "six

---

5. Walton, *Genesis One*, 58.
6. Collins, *Genesis 1–4*, 73.

workdays are a literary device to display the creation week as a careful and artful effort."⁷ Correspondingly, Richard Middleton writes, "The text, then, by its careful literary artistry, evokes a creator-God carefully constructing an artful world according to a well-thought-out plan for the benefit of creatures."⁸ As such, it suggests that the biblical author is calling attention not to a scientific process of creation (of which he knows little or nothing), nor to a literal, historical description of twenty-four hours per day. Paul Garner clarifies: "The first book of the Bible is not, in the words of the cliché, 'a scientific textbook.'"⁹ He solidifies this view by resorting to ancient culture. "If it were, how could it possibly have been understood by generations of people before modern science was developed?"[10]

The creation narrative, therefore, is not about science being in error or, conversely, the Bible not being trustworthy history. Rather, this understanding of creation should, quite simply, separate—as light does from darkness—the conflict between science and the Bible by recognizing that these two disciplines are not even in the same classroom, much less the same school. For the one—science—resides in the campus of human observation of the natural order (which God created!), while the other—the biblical account—lies in the chapel of the spirit, its architecture theology. To quote Kenton Sparks, "We will read Genesis far better if we understand it as a theological commentary on the world known to the scribes than as a description of factual history."[11]

SUMMARY

In this short chapter, two objectives were held. The first was to overview the importance of Gen 1–11, finding it to correspond to a literary prologue. The other, and more important aim was to ask, What is the literary structure of Gen 1? Having previously scanned the six-day sequence, we found within its "straightforward" six-day outline the existence of a more subtle

---

7. Collins, *Genesis 1–4*, 73.

8. Middleton, *Liberating Image*, 77.

9. Garner, *New Creationism*, 15. (MSc, Geology and Biology, University College London, specializing in paleobiology.)

10. Garner, *New Creationism*, 15.

11. Sparks, "Response to Gordon Wenham," 109. (PhD, University of North Carolina; Provost and Vice President, Academic Affairs, Eastern University.)

and elegant format, the two-panel model based on three paired days. In the coming chapters we will work from this cryptic, symmetrical structure to interpret the Genesis author's message.

CHAPTER 2

Creation Triad: Days 1 and 4

IN CHAPTER 1, TWO reading patterns were described. One was to read creation *vertically*, that is, down the story's chronologically based sequence of days. That pattern is far and away the most common approach. But it is not the only reading route though chapter 1. Nor is it, as we will come to see, the most theologically significant.

There is another and more eloquent way to read Gen 1, and that is the two-panel, three-paired day pattern. That structure reads across creation's days, connecting them, hence Days 1→4, Days 2→5, and Days 3→6. This method, then, reads the creation story horizontally.

Furthermore, when we read Gen 1, we need to recognize that this story of origins is being told not from today's scientific perspective; therefore, there is no need for today's readers to make accommodations when conflicts occur, as they will, between what we know and what the Bible states. Rather, the creation text is based on observations and beliefs of people who lived in the ancient Near East. In those societies and times, humans were not so much interested in questions of how (things came into existence) and when (things happened). What they sought to know, according to Professor John Walton, was functionality: how creation worked. Walton writes, "Consequently, to create something (cause it to exist) in the ancient world means to give it a function..."[1] As Walton closes the chapter in which this quote occurs ("Ancient Cosmology Is Function Oriented"), he states, "They thought of existence as defined by having a function in an ordered system."[2] For example, the sun functioned to bring light and warmth upon the earth.

---

1. Walton, *Genesis One*, 33.
2. Walton, *Genesis One*, 34.

Creation Triad: Days 1 and 4

As we examine Gen 1, we will find evidence that supports the contention that "creation" in the ancient world was to make, install, and establish *functions*. In other words, creation brought order to the cosmos. Thus, in our horizontal reading of the two panels, we will discover how connections between the paired days describe functionality, bringing balance and harmony where prior existed only chaos and darkness (v. 2). This leads to the text's most intriguing function, human rulership.

READING GEN 1 HORIZONTALLY

For many Christians, talk of two panels and reading the creation story horizontally is likely confusing, perhaps unsettling. Yet, having examined the story of creation, there can be no question that the biblical writer did in fact place into the text a subtle and elegant description, one formed out of two panels of thought. More so, those panels are symmetrical; that is, the work of the first three days is balanced against the completion of work in the second three days. It is that symmetry which unlocks the message found in the triadic pairing of the six days. This deliberate stylizing of the creation story requires us to ask, Why did the biblical author place into Gen 1 this two-panel, three-paired day structure? An obvious answer, in addition to mimicking creation's beauty and harmony, is that the Genesis author desires readers (and hearers of the story[3]) to make connections between the panels. To make connections, however, creation is best read horizontally rather than vertically, that is, across the panels' corresponding days. Figure 8 illustrates these two contrasting ways to approach Gen 1.

FIGURE 8. VERTICAL AND HORIZONTAL READING PATTERNS

Vertical Reading (sequentially down the days)	Horizontal Reading (across the days' connections)
Day 1 ↓ Day 6	Day 1 ⟶ Day 4 Day 2 ⟶ Day 5 Day 3 ⟶ Day 6

---

3. "It is evident in scripture that the biblical documents were written to be read aloud, often in public worship . . ." See Bible Translation Committee, "Introduction," A12.

Beyond Myth

The purpose of this chapter, therefore, is to examine the creation story through its dual-panel structure. Based on what we learned in chapter 1, figure 9 summarizes our understanding at this point.

FIGURE 9. SYMMETRICAL CONNECTIONS BETWEEN THE THREE PAIRED DAYS

Panel A	Symmetry		Panel B
Day 1	light	↔ sun/moon	Day 4
Day 2	water/air	↔ sea/sky life	Day 5
Day 3	earth/plants	↔ land life/food	Day 6

GEN 1: A STORY OF THEOLOGICAL CONNECTIONS

Our examination of the connection between Days 1 and 4 proceeds in two parts. The first is laid out in this chapter, whereas the second stage occurs in the "insert" which follows this chapter. By splitting this chapter into two segments, we will first discover how the theme of human rulership is connected to "light," and then in the following insert, we will consider the text's problematic claims surrounding "light" as described in verse 1, Day 1, and Day 4.

Light in Day 4

Of Day 4 the NIV records, "And God said, 'Let there be lights in the vault of the sky . . .'" Those "lights" consisted of the sun, the moon, and the stars. The biblical author continues, "to separate the day from the night, and let them serve as signs to mark sacred times, and days and years, and let them be lights in the vault of the sky to give light on the earth." Here the text's emphasis is on functionality, that is, on what these astral bodies do. Indeed, their function is so important that the writer twice states it. Use of repetition is characteristic of Hebrew writing style, often found in its poetry but also in the nation's prose. Figure 10 illustrates the use of repetition seen in the text's literary structuring of Day 4.

CREATION TRIAD: DAYS 1 AND 4

FIGURE 10. MICROSTRUCTURE IN DAY 4 (BASED ON NRSVUE)

Microstructure A (vv. 14–15) Organic function of the luminaries	Microstructure B (vv. 16–18) Figural function of sun and moon
1. To separate day from night (v. 14)	4. To rule the day and rule the night (v. 16)
2. To be signs and seasons (v. 14)	5. To give light on the earth (v. 17)
3. To give light on the earth (v. 15)	6. To rule over the day and the night and "to separate the light from the darkness" (v. 18)

In the first microstructure, depicted in verses 14 and 15, the luminaries have a threefold function. They separate day from night, act as signs for coming seasons, and, importantly, give actual light—that is, sunlight, moonlight, even starlight—to the earth and its creatures. This trifold function, therefore, refers to the organic nature of the luminaries, thus negating them as "gods." Yet when we come to the second microstructure in verses 16–18, much has changed. Here, these sky-objects no longer function organically as light-emitting luminaries. Rather, their function is figuratively expressed; they are described as rulers who rule over the night by bringing "light" upon the earth.

We know that humanity is the focus of this passage because the author describes functionality through a human capacity, which is rulership. To make this point, the biblical author three times uses the word "rule" in these verses. Not all Bibles, however, favor "rule." The NIV, for example, elects "govern," as does the NASB, which also footnotes "for the dominion of," whereas the ESV and the NRSVUE remain with "rule." Regardless of which word is used, the overall effect is the same: human rulership.

It is at this point that we must also notice how, in the second repetition, one of the three solar bodies has been quietly dropped from this repeating text. No longer is the author interested in stars. Furthermore, in the first telling, these three bodies were not named. But in the second telling, one is named (stars before dropping), yet the other two are cryptically labeled ("greater" and "lesser"). By not naming them, though, a controversy has stirred in today's contemporary theological world as to their meaning. It is in their labeling, however, that much of scholarship appears to miss the point that the ancient writer is making.

Responding to why the text does not name these luminaries, many commentators fall back on how the Genesis author is presenting an argument against the region's gods. That is, according to this rationale, he is loath to even mention the names "sun" and "moon" since these objects were considered sky-gods and therefore were banned—as idol worship—under Moses' commandments.

Nevertheless, there is difficulty with this line of thought, besides the obvious fact that in microstructure A, these so-called "gods" are presented as luminaries whose organic function is to emit light. But the main difficulty comes by way of the region's cultural practice of what it means to name something. In other words, the very act of naming accrues ownership or superiority over an object. Therefore, the one granting the name was considered greater than the named object. Susan Brayford observes this. "It is also odd that these two great lights with their important duties are not named by God. This would have even more strongly implied God's superiority over them."[4] This thinking, therefore, leads us to ponder the Genesis author's reason for not naming them.

In the second microstructure, however, the author has intentionally *redefined* the functionality of the sun (the "greater") and the moon (the "lesser"). Now, rather than being light-emitters he calls them "rulers." We know, of course, that astral objects do not rule, neither do they govern or exert dominion (i.e., power). However, by using words such as "rule," "govern," and "dominion," the biblical author elects to express their function through a human characteristic. In other words, these sky-bodies perform the same duties as humans, they "rule." John Walton leans into this as he writes of Day 4. "Finally we are told that their function is to govern the day and the night—the closest the text comes to personification."[5]

Indeed, Professor Walton is correct to notice the language of personification and literary comparison. Personification is a figurative means by which human characteristics are assigned to non-humans. For example, in C. S. Lewis's *Narnia* books, animals talk. Although Walton does not explore it, we will since this is the language of figurative description. More so, the text demands its exploration by virtue of the repeating microstructure.

It is at this point that we need to consider what Richard Averbeck[6] has to say. By referring to Averbeck, we add to our growing collection of literary terms, as he introduces the literary device known as *analogy*. An

---

4. Brayford, *Genesis*, 217. (PhD in Biblical Interpretation, Iliff School of Theology, University of Denver; Professor and Dean of Religious Studies, Centenary College, Shreveport, LA.)

5. Walton, *Genesis One*, 63.

6. (PhD, Dropsie University; Professor of OT and Semitic Languages, Director of PhD program, Trinity International University.)

analogy compares two or more objects by setting them upon a similarity. For example, apples to oranges (i.e., fruit) or tigers to lions (i.e., mammals). In other words, a comparison of "this" to "that." Averbeck recalls how the ancients observed the movement of astral objects and used them in their myths. He writes, "They [likely] knew they were using analogies."[7] Indeed, Averbeck applies this literary device to the entirety of Gen 1. To illustrate, he describes "a seven-day process because the creation of the cosmos was God's work, and this was God's work week, so to speak. Thus, the seven-day structure is an analogy that derives from and reinforces the regular pattern of the work week..."[8]

Richard Middleton, in his study on the *imago Dei* (Latin for "image of God"), also points to analogy, writing, "The purpose of the sun and moon is analogous..."[9] Noting the text's reliance on personification, he likens these sky-bodies' function to humanity's role in governance, which is a "royal function."[10] In citing Middleton, I do not mean to imply that he necessarily agrees with the interpretation found here. To the contrary, Middleton limits the functionality of the sun/moon to their "luminary function." Nevertheless, he does find within the sun/moon pairing that "the account of human creation on the sixth day, the portrayal of the heavenly bodies on the fourth day of creation may also be read as contributing to the affirmation of human dignity and agency."[11]

If Averbeck and Middleton are correct, then the biblical author is using the descriptive terms "greater" and "lesser" not so much to avoid naming these objects as vile sky-gods but rather for comparative and referential reasons based on functionality. If this is the case, then the function of the second microstructure, which orients to *rulership*, becomes key to understanding the biblical author's cryptic point in not naming them. Simply put, he wants readers to form a comparison. Importantly, that comparison, *expressed as an analogy about human rulership*, is tied to two ideas. One is relational; it considers which of the two is "the greater" and which is "the lesser." Thus, an analogy is formed by the comparison:

> as God is to sun (i.e., the "greater"),
> so too humanity is to moon (i.e., the "lesser").

---

7. Averbeck, "Literary Day," 13.
8. Averbeck, "Literary Day," 31.
9. Middleton, *Liberating Image*, 54.
10. Middleton, *Liberating Image*, 54.
11. Middleton, *Liberating Image*, 211.

In this case, the comparison makes use of the two most visible objects in the sky: the sun and the moon. And by means of analogy he instructs which is the greater (God) and which is the lesser (humans). The second part of the analogy is driven by personification, vesting the sky-objects with the human trait of rulership. This comparison completes the analogy:

> As the sun—the "greater"—rules over the day,
> so too does God—as the "greater"—rule;
> And
> As the moon—the "lesser"—rules over darkness,
> so too does humanity—as the "lesser"—rule.

All of this makes perfect sense if we understand the text *to be an analogy* about God as "the greater" and humanity as the "lesser," hence God's junior partner, his vice-rulers. Furthermore, this interpretation coheres nicely with other scholars, such as Westermann,[12] who find the creation phrase "image of God" to indicate human rulership.

What permits us to see it this way is Day 4's threefold use of "rule." The word "rule," being a human and not a sky-object function, is the aim of the comparison. It is most certainly not aimed at vesting vile "sky-gods" with rulership over God's creation. The biblical author is expressing God's desire to have humanity rule over the earth (as his representative). Meredith Kline, writing out of a three-paired day context, asserts, "Man is king over creation, but he is a vassal-king, he reigns as one under the Creator's authority, obligated to devote his kingdom to the Great King."[13]

Summary

We saw how Day 4's presentation was formed by two symmetrical microstructures. Both were built on the structural connection of "light." In the first use, "light" was attributed to actual light given off by the sun, the moon, and the stars. In the second microstructure, the biblical author did not employ literal language to convey meaning. Rather, he used figurative language. This was accomplished through analogy and personification. By doing so, he shifted emphasis from the sky-objects' function as luminaries

---

12. Westermann. *Genesis*, 11. "Humanity exercises sovereignty over the rest of creation."

13. Kline, *Kingdom Prologue*, 39–40. (Professor Emeritus, Westminster Seminary and Gordon-Conwell.)

casting organic light on the earth to the human function of rulership which brought "light" (i.e., wisdom in ruling) to the created order.

Further, by labeling—not naming—the sun and the moon as "the greater" and "the lesser," an analogy was formed. In it, the biblical author made the theological claim that the "sun" (a.k.a. God) is far superior to the "moon" (a.k.a. humanity). Hence, he informed Israel and the ancient world that God is superior to all other sky-bodies (i.e., "gods," of which "stars" were dropped from the text once the analogy was formed) and that Israel's God rules as the greatest ruler (as does the sun). Further, this "heavenly" ruler—whose domain is the heavenlies above—assigned humanity to be his vice-rulers, to oversee the terrestrial world's "darkness," as does the moon. The biblical writer's teaching provides a vast contrast to the region's myths, which purport humans to be servants of the gods, slaves under "their rule."

Conclusion

In our examination of Gen 1 so far, what underlies our study is how connections are being made between the creation days. Thus, the pairing of Day 1 and Day 4 leads directly from Day 1's "light" to Day 4's light-emitting bodies. However, in Day 4's second microstructure, we found an anthropocentric description that pictures the "greater" and the "lesser" lights through the analogy of human rule (see 1:26–27). Tying this together (including 1:6 and 1:14–18), Middleton finds that these texts "leads to the presumption" of a "royal function or purpose of humanity in 1:26..."[14] It is this textual direction of a royal function that we will follow in the coming chapter in which we pick up Days 3 and 6. But first, in a follow-on insert, we examine the biblical controversy over the problematic use of the word "light" in Genesis.

Gen 1 and the Problematic Use of "Light"

The word "light" is used several times in Gen 1. The first instance comes as God creates "the heavens." While the word "light" is not found in Genesis's opening verse, it is easily inferred. After all, to create "the heavens" is akin to making the majestic, cosmic light show that fills the universe. The second time "light" appears is in Day 1; here, it is also attributed to God. The text states, "And God said, 'Let there be light.'" And then the final time

14. Middleton, *Liberating Image*, 54.

"light" is taken up is in Day 4, in which God makes the sun, the moon, and the stars.

There are several problems, however, with these three usages. One is, if God "created" the universe (e.g., the "heavens") in verse 1, a universe filled with light, then why is the earth shrouded in darkness in verse 2? Another is, if God spoke "light" into the earth on Day 1, then why is it necessary to repeat the bringing forth of the sun for a second time on Day 4? After all, if in verse 1 the "heavens and the earth" were created, then clearly the sun was present, as the earth must orbit it.

Questions as these have generated much theological debate. It is at this point that we are reminded of Walter Brueggemann's statement, "Our exposition must recognize that what we have in the text is *proclamation*. The [creation] poem does not narrate 'how it happened,' as though Israel were interested in the *method* of how the world became God's world. . . . Israel is concerned with *God's lordly intent*, not his *technique*."[15]

One other point before we take up this controversy: when we turn to the creation text, the word "light" is found ten times in Gen 1. It initially appears in Day 1, in which the biblical author refers to it five times. And then again on Day 4 is this same fivefold pattern. That artistic symmetry is displayed in figure 11. Such symmetry reinforces the idea that the biblical author is not writing in a scientific genre but rather is intentionally employing figurative language to proclaim a theological message. Additionally, the word "lights," meaning "luminaries," occurs three times (vv. 14, 15, and 16).

FIGURE 11. SYMMETRICAL USAGE OF "LIGHT"

Day 1 "Light" used five times	Day 4 "Light" used five times
• Verse 3 (twice)	• Verse 15 (once)
• Verse 4 (twice)	• Verse 16 (twice)
• Verse 5 (once)	• Verse 17 (twice)

Light "In the Beginning"

As seen above, hosts of "luminaries" are implied in verse 1, a result of God having created "the heavens." Some scholars, though, read that verse as if it were an introductory statement. In other words, what we might call a topic sentence. As a topic sentence, it tells the reader that what follows in

15. Brueggemann. *Genesis*, 26.

the coming text is the story of how God went about creating the "heavens and the earth." This is different than reading the statement as though God had already engaged in an act of creation. Hence, if we follow closely the story of creation, the actual acts of creation begin on Day 1 (v. 3), and not, significantly, with verse 1's summary proclamation.

Bruce Waltke is one scholar who thinks verse 1 is a summary. As such, it anticipates God's acts of creation which follow. He offers, therefore, this translation for Gen 1:1: "In the beginning God created the cosmos. Now (this is how it happened)..."[16] By adding the implied phrase "this is how it happened," Waltke suggests that the creation statement of verse 1 is introductory. It summarizes the six-day account, which is about the Divine Being Elohim who, in the beginning, created the universe. Miller and Soden also write from this summary viewpoint, declaring, "... Genesis 1:1 gives a general statement, which will then be described in relation to the relevant parts"[17] (i.e., the following days of creation). In the technical world of biblical theologians, this view makes verse one an *independent* statement.

Continuing along that line, verse 2 instructs modern readers how the ancient world thought of the earth at the "beginning." In the ancient Near East, it was commonly considered that the earth's seas were preexistent. Of this idea, Waltke adds, "This reading also entails a pre-Genesis time and earth."[18] Thus, when we read verse 2, it confirms the ancient perception of an already-formed and water-filled earth. This is what we earlier discovered in the word-phrase *tohu bohu*. Hence, earth is completely barren, void of all functions necessary to make and sustain life. This is indicated by the deep darkness covering the seas in verse two. In that outlook, no land is yet to be seen. It is as if the earth's land were held hostage, locked up by the sea, imprisoned beneath the dark, foreboding waters.

Therefore, when verse 3 is read, we hear of a wind or spirit sent by God to survey this darkened and preexisting sea. This leads to the first act of the creation sequence, which is to eliminate darkness. This is heard as God speaks of Day 1, "Let there be light."

John Sailhamer[19] and John Walton[20] point to the word "beginning." Writing separately, they both find that "beginning" announces the start of a period of time in which creation occurs. Thus, verse one does not, as commonly thought, refer to the moment in time when creation took place.[21]

---

16. Waltke, *Dance*, 133.
17. Miller and Soden, *In the Beginning*, 85.
18. Waltke, *Dance*, 134.
19. Sailhamer, *Genesis Unbonded*, 42.
20. Walton, *Genesis One*, 43.
21. Such a view, naturally, dismisses concordists who see in verse 1 evidence

Therefore, Gen 1:1 is an introduction to a sequence of events which follow, namely, the six days of creation.

Resolving "Light's" Several Conflicts in Gen 1

Verses 1 and 2, therefore, set the stage for God's initiation of the six creation days, acts[22] which begin on Day 1. Of those acts, they often are associated with bringing "light," a word that occurs multiple times (see figure 11). However, it is in those multiple usages that many readers find this text problematic when read against today's science.

Here, Richard Averbeck adds to our understanding. He draws a distinction between sunlight (caused by the creation of the sun on Day 4) and "light" that precedes it on Day 1. He concludes that "light and sunlight are not the same in Gen 1, since the creation of the sun, moon, and stars takes place later, on Day 4."[23] Averbeck wonders, then, if the ancients "could think of the creation of 'light'"—on Day 1—as having to do *with the presence of God*"[24] (emphasis added). His rationale is based on the idea that the "light" of Day 1 is a contrast with the condition of "darkness" which covered the sea in verse two. He notes, "In fact, all the creation days in Gen 1 beginning in v. 3 are designed to eliminate the conditions of v. 2."[25] Significantly, then, it seems that both words—light (v. 3) and darkness (v. 2)—in this context are figurative and not literal expressions, holding the aim of cutting away,[26] that is, separating light from darkness.

Averbeck's observation is shared by others who write on this issue. For example, Victor Hamilton notes, "It will perhaps strike the reader of this story as unusual that its author affirms the existence of light (and a *day* for that matter) without the existence of the sun, which is still three 'days' away."[27] Kenneth Turner wonders, "Was the light of day 1 even created?"[28] He clarifies, "Gen 1:3 does not use 'create' or 'make' with reference to light; 'let there be' could refer to doing something with preexisting

---

supporting a biblical equivalence of the "Big Bang theory."

22. Some scholars refine the "six" days of creation into "eight" acts. See, for example, Middleton, *Image of God*, 76.

23. Averbeck, "Literary Day," 18.

24. Averbeck, "Literary Day," 19.

25. Averbeck, "Literary Day," 18.

26. Arnold, *Genesis*, 37 and 41. This use of "cutting away" will be revisited in chapter 8, subsection "Tree Five Times."

27. Hamilton, *Book of Genesis*, 121.

28. Turner, "Teaching Genesis 1," 199.

(divine?) light."[29] This leads to the question "Is it actually light that day 1 is addressing?"[30]

Putting these scholars together, a way forward is found by not reading Day 1's light as being sunlight or light from the cosmos. Rather, it may reflect God's own glory (light) that now illumes an earth covered in darkness (v. 2). And that, apparently, is how Jesus's disciple John saw it too. John begins his gospel with a literary prologue (vv. 1–18). Many have noted a parallel between John's opening chapter and what the Genesis author wrote. The NET comments on this similarity. "For John, the words 'In the beginning' are most likely a conscious allusion to the opening words of Genesis—'In the beginning.'"[31] Continuing, the NET records, "Other concepts which occur prominently in Gen 1 are also found in John's prologue: 'life' (1:4) 'light' (1:4) and 'darkness' (1:5)."[32]

What the NET refers to as "concepts" are mainly figurative expressions, something that characterizes John's writing. Indeed, that is precisely how he wrote of "light" and "darkness" in verse 5: "The light shines in the darkness, and the darkness has not overcome it." John, writing with Genesis chapter 1 in mind, found a theological correspondence between the creation language of Gen 1 and the coming person of Jesus Christ. Christ came, in John's view, to put away darkness by replacing it with the *"light" of God*. Because John wrote his prologue with Genesis's opening verses in mind, we may confidently put forth an interpretation that is informed by figurative and not literal language. It is, to quote Brueggemann, "proclamation."

This understanding is possible, indeed preferred, when we comprehend the purpose of the creation story. Read as a literary narrative, something Jonny Miller and John Soden advance, it is easier to discern the author's theological purpose.[33] Bruce Waltke further adds to this discussion, stating, "These obvious incongruities in the text suggest to more and more evangelicals that a literary reading of Genesis 1:2–2:3 is called for."[34]

---

29. Turner, "Teaching Genesis 1," 199.
30. Turner, "Teaching Genesis 1," 199.
31. NET, study note "a," John 1:1.
32. NET, study note "a," John 1:1.
33. Miller and Soden, *In the Beginning*, 46–47, 49.
34. Waltke, *Dance*, 137.

Beyond Myth

Conclusion

To conclude this brief insert on "light" and its cryptic,[35] that is, problematic employment in Gen 1, we find that (1) the separation of "light" from "darkness" is a creation work intention of God and that (2) Genesis's first three verses, plus Day 1 and Day 4, are imbued with figurative language; in other words, this is theological description. What this finding means and how it relates to the theme of biblical rulership will be seen in chapters 3 and 4.

---

35. See the introduction in this book, subsection "Biblical Interpretation over the Ages," for how the ancients perceived parts of Scripture as a "cryptic" text. Hendel writes, "A cryptic text has coded or hidden meanings, which is the task of the interpreter to uncover." Hendel, *Genesis*, 50.

CHAPTER 3

Creation Triad: Days 3 and 6

IN THIS CHAPTER, WE will follow the direction carved out by the analogy of the sun and moon, which alludes to the relationship between Creator and created. That telling introduces us to what "created in the image and likeness of God" means. Namely, the Heavenly King desires to establish his royal reign on this terrestrial earth. But in doing so, he determines to rule through humanity.

Throughout this book the importance of understanding the literary nature of Genesis is emphasized. This is evident, for example, when viewing Gen 1 as comprised of three pairs of connected workdays consolidated within two "panels." Scholars refer to this description as "literary artistry" set within a "literary framework." In this chapter, that artistic framework is conceptualized as a *mosaic of theological thought*. Importantly, like a mosaic, it is best perceived by conforming the text's individual pieces into one overall picture.

In this chapter, therefore, we continue our study of the paired workdays by taking up the connection between Days 3 and 6. That allows discovery of how Day 6 is the literary peak of the creation week, pointing as it does to the creation of humanity in God's image and likeness. By then returning to Day 4, the specific purpose for being created in God's image comes into view, namely human rulership over darkness.

CONNECTING DAYS 3 AND 6

Day 3 reads in part:

> Then God said, "Let the land produce vegetation: seed-bearing plants and trees on the land that bear fruit with seed in it, according to their various kinds." And it was so (v. 11).

The formation of the earth's vegetation is the final work described in Panel A. Importantly, the covering of the land's surface with vegetation provides food for Panel B's inhabitants. That purpose is discovered as the author writes of Day 6 in verse 29:

> Then God said, "I give you every seed-bearing plant on the face of the whole earth and every tree that has fruit with seed in it. They will be yours for food. And to all the beasts of the earth and all the birds in the sky and all the creatures that move along the ground—everything that has the breath of life in it—I give every green plant for food." And it was so.

Days 3 and 6, therefore, point to an obvious connection in which God is provisioning the earth as a storehouse for the planet's life forms. With that relationship between those days established, we now turn to Day 6 and its focus on humanity.

Day 6: Literary Structure

Day 6's workday spans Gen 1:24–31, ending at 2:1. How the biblical author structures this important day is outlined in figure 12.

FIGURE 12. STRUCTURE OF THE SIXTH DAY

1:24–25	1:26–28	1:29–31
God made animal life from out of the land	God creates humanity	God gives food to all land life

Once again, the biblical author presents content through three structural segments. Of these, the formation of humanity is most important. In the world of biblical scholarship, the words "peak," "high point," and sometimes "climax" are used to identify a passage's most important part.

Creation Triad: Days 3 and 6

C. John Collins writes, "The 'peak' is that part of the narrative that has the maximum interest..."[1]

Applying Collins to our outline of Day 6, of its three content clusters, the creation of humanity is clearly the most significant. Hence, verses 26–28 form the "peak" of Day 6's creation activity. Further earning that conclusion is the author's use of poetry. By inserting poetry into the middle of verses 26–28, the author forthrightly signals his intent, which is to show that humanity is held in esteem far above Day 6's non-human counterparts. Verse 27 declares:

> So God created mankind in his own image,
> in the image of God he created them;
> male and female he created them.

Created in His Image

The story of humanity's creation is framed on three related layers of thought. This triad, formed out of verses 26, 27, and 28, may be imagined as a triangular shape. Verse 26, as one of the triangle's base points, declares God's intention to make humanity in his image and likeness for the express purpose of ruling over all land animals. While verses 26 and 28 are written in prose, the biblical author turns to poetry to stress the importance of verse 27, proclaiming the creation of humanity. Completing this triad is verse 28, which approximates verse 26 with its emphasis on rule.

Therefore, this singular use of poetry must not be missed. Through it the writer points to the passage's peak question, namely, what does it mean to be created in God's image? Not leaving this important question to chance interpretation, the Genesis writer ensures his readers' understanding by intentionally blending style, genre, and structure. This is displayed in figure 13.

When we look at figure 13, we can visualize how the author wraps the twice-used word "image" (v. 27) within the twice-employed word "rule" (vv. 26 and 28). That structural practice is sometimes referred to as "sandwiching"[2] or "bracketing." Read that way, the phrase "God created mankind in his own image" is defined by this rulership context. This is supported by Victor Hamilton, who writes, "In God's eyes, all of mankind

---

1. Collins, *Genesis 1–4*, 20.
2. Brodie, *Genesis as Dialogue*, 195.

is royal."³ Expanding on this idea, and writing out of a context involving Ps 72, which is considered a "royal" psalm, Hamilton asserts of the psalm writer's "king" that he is "the champion of the poor and the disadvantaged. What is expected of the king is responsible care over that which he rules."⁴ Hamilton succinctly states, "Man is created to rule. But this rule is to be compassionate and not exploitative."⁵

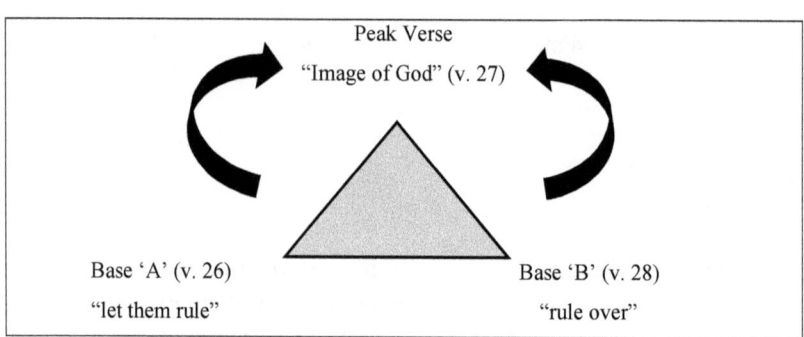

FIGURE 13. BRACKETING THE "IMAGE OF GOD"

Meaning of "Created in His Image and Likeness"

Without question, there are many ways to understand the rather cryptic creation phrase, "in the image of God." Tremper Longman acknowledges such while at the same time arguing that "a strong case can be made that we should understand 'image' here in a way that it is used elsewhere [i.e., in the ancient world], namely, for statues that represent the king in his realm."⁶ Furthermore, he connects the imagery of a statute, which represents a royal throne, to the Genesis statement of humanity's creation. He writes, "Men and women are created to represent God's presence and authority . . ."⁷ Thereby, Longman picks up on the relationship between being made in

---

3. Hamilton, *Book of Genesis*, 135. (PhD, Mediterranean Studies, Brandeis University; Professor of Bible and Theology, Asbury Seminary.) Also see Westermann, *Genesis*, 10–11.

4. Hamilton, *Book of Genesis*, 138.

5. Hamilton, *Book of Genesis*, 138.

6. Longman, "What Genesis 1–2 Teaches," 111.

7. Longman, "What Genesis 1–2 Teaches," 111.

Creation Triad: Days 3 and 6

God's image and God's rulership. In other words, statues were often placed throughout a kingdom to remind everyone of the realm's ruler. Similarly, humans—as bearers of God's image—are living statues whose presence recalls to all that earth is God's creation, and he has determined to rule through his appointed "living statues" (i.e., humanity as viceroy).

When the creation text is examined within the context of verses 26–28, one overriding assertion is irrefutable: rulership. In a deep look at that connection, Richard Middleton concludes that "the *imago Dei* refers to humanity's office and role as God's earthly delegates, whose terrestrial task is analogous to that of the heavenly court."[8] Here, reference to a heavenly court and a terrestrial commission stem, in part, from Middleton's comparative look at Ps 8. Continuing, Middleton writes, "In 1:26–28, that task is understood as the exercise of significant power over the earth and its nonhuman creatures..."[9] He summarizes, "Imaging God thus involves representing and perhaps extending in some way God's rule on earth through the ordinary communal practices of human sociocultural life."[10]

Middleton's ending remark, "human sociocultural life," directly refers to rulership within the human community and through its daily, that is, its "ordinary" routines and roles. Importantly, Middleton understands that the concept of "rulership" is not limited to just a designated personage such as King David but is equally applied with vigor to all of God's human subjects. In the kingdom of God there is no one of privilege: all are equal; all possess the gift of being created in God's image. And all bear the responsibility of being God's rulers through the course of their lives.

How that rule is to occur often finds pithy elaborations in many psalms and proverbs and is foundational for Christ's kingdom parables and teachings. To illustrate, Jesus prefers those who are poor in spirit, as he does the meek. Pacemakers fill his kingdom as do those whose hearts are pure, concluding that to such "is the kingdom of heaven." Human rulership, then, if it is to image God to the world, must function for the welfare of others. To demonstrate this the psalmist crisply writes, "Blessed are those who act justly, who always do what is right" (106:3).

Returning to Middleton, he pairs understanding of the image of God as being "representational" and "representative." He considers representational

---

8. Middleton, *Liberating Image*, 60.
9. Middleton, *Liberating Image*, 60.
10. Middleton, *Liberating Image*, 60.

as a "similarity or analogy between God and humans."[11] This mirrors the statements above and relates directly to the sun/moon analogy of the previous pairing of Day 1 and 4, in which God and humanity are joined together much like the cosmic dance of sun and moon. In that ballet, the function of humanity is to reflect to the world God's glory. One way is through worship. The other is to serve as God's representative. Hence, humanity is entrusted to administer "the earthly realm on God's behalf."[12]

Stephen Dempster uses words much like Middleton. He acknowledges that 1:26–28 describes humanity as having a unique pairing with God. Here, Dempster elects "relational" and "referential," citing of humanity that "their being automatically signifies God."[13] Dempster goes on, noting how the biblical words "image" and "likeness" indicate a royal status for the race. "The male and female as king and queen of creation are to exercise rule over their dominion, the extent of which is the entire earth."[14]

Vertically Linking Day 4 and Day 6

At this point, we return to the sun/moon analogy of Day 4. In it we found that God, as analogous to the "sun," is identified through the label-word "greater." Conversely, humanity was likened to the "moon," designated under the descriptive label "lesser." The point the biblical writer makes is that humanity is always and forever the "lesser" when compared to the Divine Creator. Second, not only is this a referential analogy—that is, lesser to greater—but it is relational. Humanity is forever linked to God since he is the Creator, and we, as Day 6 declares, are made in his image. In that relationship of superior to subordinate, God assigns rulership roles. The text reads of the sun (God) that it is to "govern the day," while the moon (humanity) is to "govern the night."

Here, by vertically combining Day 4 with Day 6, we come upon the genesis of the grand yet tragic biblical theme of human rulership. Thus Middleton writes, "In the context of the Genesis 1 creation story it appropriately symbolizes the beginning of the rule of the human race."[15] Here, then, is humanity's royal coronation, which charges humans with

11. Middleton, *Liberating Image*, 88.
12. Middleton, *Liberating Image*, 88.
13. Dempster, *Dominion and Dynasty*, 58.
14. Dempster, *Dominion and Dynasty*, 59.
15. Middleton, *Liberating Image*, 212.

creation-care under God's sovereign reign. In the analogy of the sun and moon, humans are called to rule "over the night." To determine what that means, we may draw an inference from Gen 1:2 and its description of "darkness," which was the primordial condition of an earth whose land lay "captured" under the sea's all covering waters. At this point we need to recall Richard Averbeck, who wrote, "According to Gen 1, God progressively through the six creation days eliminated the totally dark and watery unformed and unfilled conditions of v. 2. Moreover, darkness, as opposed to light, is often used as a metaphor for evil or catastrophe in Scripture..."[16] Significantly, it is that "darkness" which humanity, as analogically pictured as the "lesser," has been ordained to rule over. How that frames out is revealed in Days 2 and 5, seen in the next chapter.

Concluding, we return to a previous quote from Victor Hamilton, who laid down the ethical standard for human rule, namely "to be compassionate and not exploitative."[17] Hence, humans are to image God through the royal function of rulership in the same manner as God, who is the creator. Rulership is to be guided by providing for others as God did in making earth a sacred place for all life. Humanity is charged with the well-being of all of God's children. Human rule, therefore, must aspire to the welfare and provisioning of the race, providing sustenance, whether that is food (see Day 3), medical care, or shelter. This is God's ethical demand as imprinted on his vice-regents. Rather than engage in warfare, with its aim to take and destroy, humans are to emphasize God's gifts of care and life. In that commissioning there is no place for lies and deception, or for harm and hurt, as this referentially created race engages in rulership. To say this simply, the standard for ethical rulership is set upon the race's being created in the goodness of God's image.

SUMMARY

In this chapter, by applying literary structure, author style, and ancient culture to Gen 1, a theological interpretation of the pairing of Days 3 and 6 was formed. Drawing on personification and analogy, we were able to connect Day 4's sun and moon analogy—expressed as rulers—to Day 6's creation of humanity in the image and likeness of God, who is the supreme Ruler. Out of that we uncovered the theme of human rulership, whose function is

---

16. Averbeck, "Ancient Near Eastern Mythography," 350.
17. Hamilton, *Book of Genesis*, 138.

to rule over earth's darkness. Yet that rule must be directed by compassion, not intolerance; by freedom, not enslavement; and by peace, not hatred. Further, by linking Day 4 with Day 6, we returned to reading the text vertically. In other words, by assembling the various pieces of the creation text—whether read horizontally or vertically—Scripture's architectural shape as *a mosaic of theological thought* is affirmed.

Literary Artistry and Numbers as Ancient Communication

Ancient Israel was accustomed to the intertwining of textual features to shade meaning, for example, the blending of literary structure with author style, or how social drama provided spoken arguments a theater on which to indict the nation's priestly and governing rulers. Over time, Israel became used to messages that were communicated in various ways. This can be seen as her prophets acted out dramatic scenes, often pointing out intolerable social practices and corrupt religious leaders. One illustration is how God commanded Ezekiel to place before the people a large clay tablet and upon it render Jerusalem complete with siege ramps. In the end, he was to lie next to it, foretelling a coming and horrendous future (see Ezek 4). And then there was Hosea, whom God told to take as a wife the prostitute Gomer, an allusion that confronted the people with their own spiritual adultery, while also communicating "God's divine compassion and the love that will not let Israel go."[18]

Readers, listeners, and observers learned to decode and decipher these stylized forms of communication. Whereas we struggle and fight over hermeneutics and a text's plain sense pitted against figurative meaning, that was not how ancients looked upon (or heard or witnessed) Scripture. Indeed, while we see Genesis as "straightforward," Israel would likely have understood it as literary artistry. Certainly, many of the church's founding fathers and mothers did, as well as many current scholars and Bible teachers. Bruce Waltke, in citing another scholar, "claim[s] that Scripture is at least a magnificent literary-artistic representation of the creation."[19] What Waltke holds in mind is the two-panel, three-paired day construction of Gen 1.

Tremper Longman makes a case for reading the text as a literary artifice.[20] This view of Scripture navigates the tension between the plain

---

18. Introduction to book of Hosea, *Oxford Annotated Bible, Revised Standard Version* © 1965, 1088.

19. Waltke, *Dance*, 171–72.

20. Longman, "Storytellers and Poets," 137–49.

Creation Triad: Days 3 and 6

sense of a text's wording and its sophisticated literary structure. Thus, the creation story becomes not so much history per se, as it is a story of God's proclamations, which are enunciated through symbol, representation, and metaphor. Longman finds, therefore, that Genesis "is not attempting to be as close as possible to a dispassionate reporting of events. Rather we have proclamation, with the result that the history is shaped to differing degrees."[21] Denis Lamoureux sees within the text's symmetry a kind of poetic expression. He states, "The correct and most basic definition of the term 'poetry' simply means 'structured writing.'"[22]

Claims such as these return us to the many points of view held by ancient writers who frequently combined literary structure with author style to form poetic and prose expression. That eloquent blend brought about a message that current generations of Bible readers, set upon a text's literalness, often fail to consider or even see. This is particularly evident in the Genesis author's employment of numbers. Bruce Waltke, referring to Umberto Cassuto, notes "the conscious, not coincidental, use of the important number seven along with the numbers three and ten to structure our text and to determine many of its details. Embedded in ancient Near East literatures the number six represents incompleteness and the number seven represents resolution, wholeness, completeness."[23]

By these remarks, Waltke and Cassuto do what most scholars avoid, which is attach meaning to numerical values. As we go forward in this creation series, we will continue to encounter the Genesis author's use of numbers to inform his message. Though, in many instances, we won't know precisely what such numbers might have meant; nevertheless, that should not hinder us from making a good faith attempt to infer number-meaning based on context.

In the ancient world, numbers took on meaning far beyond literal value. That thought may be inferred by a statement made by Joseph Colson, who wrote, "Numbers are not the key to everything in the Bible, but they are important."[24] Cassuto writes of the number seven, "It was the number of perfection . . . and particular importance attached to it in the symbolism of numbers."[25]

We have already glimpsed this "symbolism" with the number *seven*, which denotes sacredness, perfection, and, per Bruce Waltke,

---

21. Longman, "Storytellers and Poets," 146.
22. Lamoureux, *Ancient Science*, 164.
23. Waltke, *Dance*, 170.
24. Coleson, *Genesis 1–11*, 175.
25. Cassuto, *Commentary on Genesis*, 12.

completeness.[26] But other than the well-known (or infamous) 666, which is the "sign" or "mark of the beast," few of today's readers realize how extensively Scripture employs what may be termed number-meaning. Yet, numbers are so intertwined with meaning that they shift comprehension of a text from literal to figurative. In other words, numbers forced upon a reader/listener an additional avenue from which to comprehend the sacred scrolls. One way that numbers accomplish this is to act like a conveyor belt, connecting one part of a text to another. In that sense, it is not so much a precise meaning held by a number but rather the use of like numbers to link one biblical event to another. For example, the number four,[27] or some form of it, such as forty, draws a connection between Moses at Sinai and Christ in the wilderness.[28]

To undertake that connectivity, this study has been following a plan of discovery that first permits seeing how the biblical author employed numbers and symmetry in a text's construction. For example, we have already noted this in the two-panel, three-paired-day structure. Another example is to observe how often words and phrases were repeated, such as "good" *seven* times or "created" *three* times. Once we are familiar with Scripture's stylistic employ of numbers, then in book 2 of this series we will consolidate that usage, postulating a table of meaning. But first we need to continue seeing the forest, that is, to form a larger snapshot of how frequently the author used numbers before we designate specific interpretations.

To recap, many biblical scholars find Genesis's symmetrical construction to be a type of poetic expression, an artistic communication in which numbers give rise not only to a structural system[29] (such as the two-panel format) but are used stylistically, augmenting textual meaning as well. Simply stated, biblical numbers comprise one component of an ancient author's written style. In doing so, numbers take on representational values far beyond their use as mere digits.

---

26. Waltke, *Dance*, 170.

27. See Moberly on the number four or forty. Moberly, *Theology of Genesis*, 105.

28. See Exod 24:18 and Matt 4:2.

29. Cassuto writes of Gen 1, "The structure of our section is based on a system of numerical harmony." Cassuto, *Commentary on Genesis*, 12.

CHAPTER 4

Creation Triad: Days 2 and 5

To understand the connection between Days 2 and 5, it is necessary to read this account as might an ancient Israelite. Importantly, that perspective is not based on twenty-first-century science; in contrast, we need to comprehend how those days reflect the mythology of the ancient world. We begin this chapter, therefore, by describing God's work from Day 2, after which a new literary structure, termed the "formula pattern," is examined. That construction surfaces two striking omissions in the creation story of Day 2. In search of reasons for such mysterious lapses, we will venture on to Day 3. Following resolution, the connection that links Days 2 and 5 will be identified. But in doing so yet another mystery is encountered, one tied to a contemporary debate over the translation of the Hebrew word *tanninim*. In the end, we will discover that God's work during these days leads to two conclusions. First, Elohim is engaged in making earth into a sacred place, and second, evil is to be confined by human rulership through God's appointment of the race as his vice regents.

THE MYSTERY BEHIND DAY 2

Of Day 2, the NRSVUE translates:

> And God said, "Let there be a dome in the midst of the waters, and let it separate the waters from the waters." So God made the dome and separated the waters that were under the dome from the waters that were above the dome. And it was so. God called the dome Sky. And there was evening and there was morning, the second day. (1:6–8)

Beyond Myth

To understand this creation work, it is helpful to return to Gen 1:2, which says, "Now the earth was formless and empty, darkness was over the surface of the deep, and the Spirit of God was hovering over the waters." In response to that darkened condition, God, on Day 1, filled the earth with light. Then, on Day 2, the planet's all-covering waters were separated into two halves, an upper half and a lower half. In this act God made a "dome" or what the NIV terms "vault," of which other Bibles declare "firmament."

Many Bible scholars believe that this dome/vault/firmament is earth's atmosphere, its air. What is important to note, however, is the placement of the waters. Part of the waters are placed atop the earth's air; the other part remains below, that is, at sea level. At the conclusion of Day 2's work, God names this upper half; it is called "sky." Yet he does not name the lower half (i.e., the seas), waiting until Day 3 to do so. This leads to a mystery: why did God not also name the seas on Day 2 as he did the sky?

Those living in the ancient world would immediately understand the importance of naming these two parts of the earth. That was due to an ancient Near Eastern belief that to name something was to gain superiority over it. In other words, the named object, in this case "sky," was now owned, or controlled, by God. Furthermore, that act would further stake out God's claim that he was superior to any life form (i.e., "gods") who might dwell in that dome space. Here, we recall how the ancient world believed that the now separated waters "above" were occupied by gods. Furthermore, those waters were held in place by something like a giant reservoir, chambers[1] out of which rain and precipitation fell upon the earth below, released through the activity of sky "gods."

Importantly, Elohim's act of installing the air by separating the waters was done without force. God did not have to resort to some type of divine combat to complete this, or any of his acts of creation, as if to wrench it away from some other god. Yet, in some ancient myths—such as *Enuma Elish*—creation occurred after a cosmic battle. Thus, by the end of the second day, the Genesis writer is making the claim that Elohim has such might and power that he can do what he wants and no "god" can resist his creative initiative.

---

1. Arnold, *Genesis*, 41. (PhD, Hebrew Union College–Jewish Institute of Religion; Paul S. Amos Professor of OT Interpretation, Asbury Theological Seminary.)

Creation Triad: Days 2 and 5

Literary Structure

God's act of naming the sky returns us to literary structure. Bill Arnold, among other scholars, finds within each day's description numerous phrases that are repeated over and over throughout the workweek. He refers to this collection as "formulaic structure."[2] In this book the terms "formula pattern" and "formula structure" are used instead. Examples of phrases which comprise this pattern are "and God said," "there was evening and morning," and "the Nth Day." In total, Arnold discerns seven phrases.[3] More so, Arnold contends that these phrases are "the most prominent literary feature in Gen 1 . . . [with] its recurring formulaic structure."[4]

Here, Arnold's reference to "recurring" depicts the structure's fluidness. It is that fluidness which permits the Genesis author to not be "bound"[5] or forced to use every phrase in describing each day's work. This results in some workdays having some but not all seven phrases found in the "formula pattern." While Arnold considers that normal, however, the absence of phrases might signal something else, such as an interpretative twist. At the very least, it should cause readers to wonder why the writer omitted certain parts of the formula pattern.

Thus, we must wonder about Day 2's two omissions. First, although God did name the space between the waters "sky," he did not name the waters below (which he delayed until Day 3). Second, and perhaps of even greater consequence, is the omission of the formula phrase "God saw that it was good."

Of all the days, it is only Day 2 that is not assessed "good." This omission is so grave we must consider its absence intentional. Hence, we must ponder the question, Why is it that God objects to using the word "good" to cap the second day's work? Why is Day 2 not worthy of being called "good"? Strangely, it is on Day 3 that both mysteries find answers. Therefore, the "fluidness" of the formula pattern (represented by Day 2's omissions) leads to solutions in the telling of Day 3. Significantly, these solutions are tied to the biblical writer's ongoing theme of human rulership.

---

2. Arnold, *Genesis*, 30.
3. Arnold, *Genesis*, 31.
4. Arnold, *Genesis*, 30.
5. Arnold, *Genesis*, 30.

Day 3's Solutions

Of God's work on Day 3, the text records in part:

> And God said, "Let the water under the sky be gathered to one place, and let dry ground appear." And it was so. God called the dry ground "land," and the gathered waters he called "seas." And God saw that it was good. (Gen 1:9–10)

In Day 3's work, God rectifies the two omissions from Day 2. Here, he names the waters "seas" but only after he first names the ground, which has now appeared, "land." After this, Elohim asserts that Day 3's work is "good." Indeed, he doubles down and twice uses the word "good," the second time affirming the land's production of food-bearing plants and trees. Hence, God's work of separating the waters leads directly to the freeing of the submerged land, which, having lain "captive" beneath the covering seas, now rises into view, thus forming the climax moment for all the work described in Panel A.

It can be seen, then, that as God "gathered" the waters into one place, what resulted was the emergence of earth's land. But not just "land": the text modifies this reference to "ground" by using the adjective "dry"; hence, a "dry ground" rises out of the saturating seas. Which, of course, is problematic, this rising up of a "dry" land from a seabed soaked in seawater.

The "Dry" Ground

The importance of calling land "dry" is rooted in Israel's theologically shaped history. This qualifier is understood by the context in which "dry ground" occurs; normally it is set within a sacred context. To illustrate, immediately following the freeing of the twelve tribes from four hundred years of enslavement in Egypt, the fleeing people find themselves pinned between the Red Sea (that is, the Sea of Reeds) and the hotly pursuing, vengeance-seeking warriors of Pharaoh. Temporarily protected by God's "tower of fire," a sacred avenue of escape is provided by the Divine Being. This occurs as Moses holds up outstretched hands, opening a channel through the waters. The text reads, "But the Israelites went through the sea on dry ground, with a wall of water on their right and on their left" (Josh 3:17).

Creation Triad: Days 2 and 5

Specific use of "dry ground" occurs again, such as when Joshua leads the twelve tribes across the Jordan near Jericho. In a picture-image replay of the Red Sea's crossing, the text once again describes the land as "dry ground." In the latter, the dry ground is contextualized by the presence of priests carrying the ark of the covenant. In other words, the ark represents the holiness of God's presence, just as Moses' outstretched hands symbolizes dependence on God's saving power. Both stories are hinged to God's sacred presence.

Yet, even before these actions take place, there is one which precedes, and that comes as Moses stands before God in Horeb, on the "mountain of God." The text records, "Take off your sandals, for the place where you are standing is holy ground" (Exod 3:5). The command to remove sandals, as the NET indicates, was done "because God was in this place, the ground was different—it was holy."[6]

These three instances recall Gen 1:2's description of earth's ground that was covered and hidden from sight by a deep and watery darkness. In the mythology of the ancient Near East, the covering seas were home to innumerable gods, such as Yam (or at times spelled Yamm). But as the Genesis creation story advances from one day to the next, it progressively reveals how God is uncovering that darkness, replacing it with the divine light of verse 3. It seems, then, that God did not name the sea "good" in Day 2 until the ground was released from its seabed captivity on Day 3. Once freed, the land was described not only as "good" but more importantly "dry," since all traces of the saturating sea water were removed, leaving the land completely "dry," free from any influence of the sea's mythical gods.

In other words, the wet ground was transformed from darkness, and in ancient Israel's way of thinking, rid of the sea's implied toxic evil and opposition to God; it was rendered pure (i.e., holy), no longer saturated by seawater that was home to the gods. Walton pictures occupants of the ancient seas as "threats" to the created "order." He views sea-born dwellers (and here he cites "the great creatures of the sea") as enemies, those who "inhabited" a domain outside of the created order. Yet, they are, as is everything, under the control of God.[7] At the conclusion of God's work on Day 3, the modifier "dry" is twice found. That twice-stated word

---

6. See NET, study note "u," Exod 3:5.

7. All references to John Walton in this paragraph come from his initial book in the *Lost World* series. See Walton, *Genesis One*, 65–66.

emphatically affirms God's work in Panel A as a holy labor, thereby making earth into a sacred site. Here we also note that the word "good" appears seven times in the creation work week, which recalls for us how *seven* signifies "sacredness."

DAY 5—CREATION AND *TANNINIM*

Day 5 records,

> And God said, "Let the water teem with living creatures, and let birds fly above the earth across the vault of the sky." So God created the great creatures of the sea and every living thing with which the water teems and that moves about in it, according to their kinds, and every winged bird according to its kind. And God saw that it was good. God blessed them and said, "Be fruitful and increase in number and fill the water in the seas, and let the birds increase on the earth." And there was evening, and there was morning—the fifth day. (Gen 1:20–30)

The connection between Days 2 and 5 is immediately presented to readers in Day 5's account. It centers upon the placement of life into the now-formed sky and the "water in the sea." In these environments the water is directed to teem with life and the sky to be filled with flying creatures. There is a mystery here, however, found in the biblical writer's use of "water" and "seas." Hence, Elohim directs marine life to fill the "water in the seas." All of which makes readers wonder about this phrase "water in the seas." Even more strange in this filling up of the two environments, air and marine, is how the writer points to one specific class of life, which is, as the NIV records, "the great creatures of the sea."

Thus, we find, just as Day 2 presented a mystery of why God named the sky above but not the sea below, so too does Day 5 hold a mystery surrounding the sea. Yet this mystery is not driven by omissions from the formula structure. Rather it is held within a contemporary debate over how to translate the Hebrew word *tanninim*. That word is found in the phrase "so God created the great creatures of the sea . . ." Yet not all Bibles agree with this selection for *tanninim*, preferring various word choices as shown in figure 14.

Creation Triad: Days 2 and 5

Figure 14. Translating "*tanninim*"

Translations for verse 21 (*tanninim*)	Found in
Great creatures of the sea	NIV
Great sea beasts	REB
Great sea creatures	ESV, NASB, NCB, NET, OJB
Great sea monsters	NRSVUE, NASB ('95), RSV
Huge whales	The Message

As figure 14 reveals, there is no consistent or favored way *tanninim* is translated in English Bibles. Victor Hamilton writes on this issue: "Much discussion has focused on the identity of the enormous marine creatures (Heb. *tanninim*, v. 21)."[8] Indeed, translators publish *tanninim* in a variety of ways. Hence, to unravel Day 5's mystery of the distinction between "water" and "sea" we first must attend to the translation debate over the word *tanninim*, which is the huge marine life form that dwells in the sea's waters.

In the selection of "great sea monsters" for *tanninim*, as in the NRSVUE, an argument is made for a translation that leans more closely to the cultural context of ancient Israel. This is seen in how Israel used the term "sea monster" to denote opposition to God. The NET elaborates in a footnote, "In Isaiah 27:1 the word is used to describe a mythological sea creature that symbolizes God's enemies."[9]

Further connecting the use of "sea monster" with Day 5's huge aquatic is Ps 104:26. In this "creation" psalm, the NET appears to duck the possibility that God created a "sea monster"—hence a mythological creature—electing instead, "Here swims the whale you made to play in it [the sea's water]." Yet, in a translator note the NET states, "Elsewhere Leviathan is a multiheaded sea monster that symbolizes forces hostile to God (see Ps 74:14; Isa 27:1), but here it appears to be an actual marine creature created by God, probably some type of whale."[10] That statement acknowledges this marine life has been created by God. But apparently the NET is not inclined to translate it as "Leviathan," a mythological creature, likely due to the Psalm's "creation context." Both the NIV and the NASB, like the NRSVUE, do however translate "Leviathan." Regarding the close relationship between

---

8. Hamilton, *Book of Genesis*, 129.
9. NET, footnote "aq," 1:21.
10. NET, translator note "ai," Ps 104:26.

Beyond Myth

Day 5 and Ps 104, Jon Levenson finds a "genetic" connection. He writes, "Only in this Psalm is Leviathan said to have been a creature of YHWH, a point that recalls the special mention in Genesis 1:21 of the creation . . . of the great sea monsters on day five."[11] Given this, we elect to use "great sea monsters" for *tanninim* since the use of that word, in the development of Israel's nationhood, associated it with those who were opposed to God and saw Israel as an enemy state.

It is here that we need to recall how N. T. Wright looked upon the sea as code for evil. He wrote, referring to the book of Revelation (13:1) and its apocalypse-stylized language, "The sea has become a dark, fearsome, threatening place from which evil emerges, threatening God's people."[12] In this regard, we also need to recall that to the peoples of the ancient Near East, the sea was viewed as primordial. That is, it is already in existence when the creation account begins, and nowhere in the text does God claim to create it.[13] However, as one reads throughout the Bible, especially in the Prophets, the ancient "sea" becomes code for chaos, evil, and forces that violently sought to undo God's "good" creation. Most immediately this will be seen in Gen 6 and the flood story. Of that, more will be discussed in the second book of this series.

With reference to antiquity and sea monsters in place, we return to the question of why the biblical writer singled out this controversial marine life form. In doing so, we must notice that the word "create" is also tied to the sea monster, as the NRSVUE states, "So God created the great sea monsters." It appears, then, that the Genesis writer is intentionally signaling the importance of this aquatic. It may surprise many, but in all the "creating" work described in Gen 1, there are only *three* instances in which the word "created" is employed. And one of these occurs here, in Day 5's creation of the "great sea monsters." Such specific use of "created" indicates a deliberate choice by the Genesis author. It seems the writer has gone out of his way to call attention to this sea creature. This is seen in figure 15.

---

11. Levenson, *Persistence of Evil*, 57.
12. Wright, *Surprised by Scripture*, 109.
13. See Levenson, *Persistence of Evil*, 57.

Creation Triad: Days 2 and 5

Figure 15. "Created" Brackets "Sea Monsters"

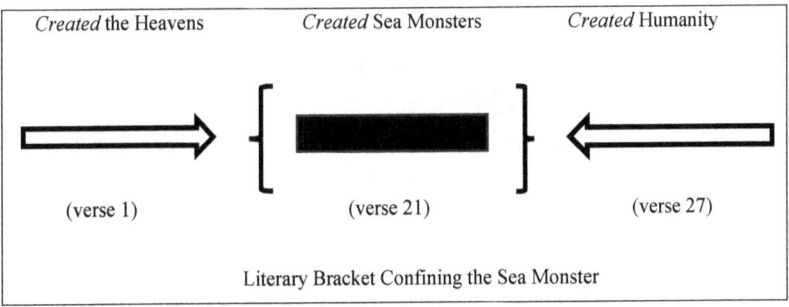

Literary Bracket Confining the Sea Monster

Figure 15 displays the word "created" as though forming a literary bracket around the sea monster. Encasement of the sea monster is formed by pairing the God who "created" the heavens and earth (v. 1) with human beings, who were "created" in his image (v. 27). In other words, the great fish—highlighted by the word "created"—has been placed under the authority of rulership, both divine and human. On one side of the "created" bracket stands God; he is firmly in control of the monstrous marine life form. On the other side is humanity, shown at the conclusion of Gen 2 as a united couple, that is, man and wife who are united under God. They are depicted, then, as occupying the second flank, across from God, and together forming a bridgehead that exerts rule and control over this great aquatic.

At this point it is helpful to turn to Jon Levenson. He begins by referring to a passage in Job chapter 40 in which the sea monster (who is presented as Leviathan) is shown to be not much more than a child's bathroom toy for God. Levenson writes how the great fish is now "merely a plaything of his divine captor."[14] Yet, in Israel's ancient world, the sea monster was viewed by the nation's prophets as a symbol for evil and Israel's enemies. Not exactly the stuff of a child's toy.

Therefore, a certain kind of tension exists for ancient readers between the "good" environment in which God created the sea monster and how Israel symbolized "sea monsters" to indicate evil. It is within this point of tension that the Genesis author uses literary structure to picture God's sovereign control and humanity's role as earthly rulers (see figure 15). Just as God created the sea monsters "good" (v. 21), so too must humanity keep creation safe, that is, "good," by not allowing the sea monster (i.e., resident

---

14. Levenson, *Persistence of Evil*, 17.

figure of opposition) to escape into the sea's dark abode. For it is there, in the deep and dark sea, that evil resides. Of this Jon Levenson writes, "The survival of Leviathan in captivity parallels the psalmist's earlier statement that God set bounds that the primeval waters must not dare to cross."[15] Levenson continues, forcefully stating, "In each case, the confinement of chaos rather than its elimination is the essence of creation."[16]

Levenson's statement, though controversial, is precisely how the Genesis author portrays the sea monster of Day 5. Created as "good," this marine life form is depicted as hemmed in, bracketed between God's reign and humanity's charge as vice-rulers. The text's literary structure, revealed through the bracketing of figure 15, points to the importance of keeping this mythological beast—symbolically an enemy—captive and at bay. Simply stated, it must not be allowed to escape into the deep and dark "sea." We find this as God blesses all marine life—including the sea monster—heard as the biblical author writes, "Be fruitful and increase in number and fill the water in the seas."

Here, we must address the phrase "the water in the seas." It is not to marine life found living within the deep, dark, and encompassing sea that God extends his blessing but only to marine life found dwelling in God's sacred environment—that is, "in the water in the seas." So, the biblical author differentiates between "sea" and "the water in the seas." This is much like we previously saw in the differentiation between "salty water" and "sweet water" found in *Enuma Elish*. Hence, in verse 2 it is the sacred wind/spirit that is pictured as hovering over the "face" (or surface layer) of the "waters."

In this mythologically referenced message, one that an ancient reader would grasp, humanity is charged with containing evil, keeping the sea monster hemmed in, pinned between God and humanity. Left in that state, it was last seen innocently frolicking in the "water in the seas," unable to escape into the abyss of the primordial ocean. Read this way, we find Elohim tasking humanity with an ominous mission. It is a challenge that will become a tipping point for the race once the story of creation moves into the garden, namely the containment of evil, or if you prefer, the continuation and advancement of goodness. Here, then, is this important tie to Day 4's personification with its rulership analogy.

---

15. Levenson, *Persistence of Evil*, 17.
16. Levenson, *Persistence of Evil*, 17.

Creation Triad: Days 2 and 5

HUMAN RULERSHIP AND THE SACRED

At this point we need to draw together what was learned from the other two paired days of the creation story, Days 1 and 4 and Days 3 and 6. Further, reading Days 4 and 6 as forming a *vertical* pair, we saw how they introduced the theme of human rulership. The biblical author accomplished this by analogy ("greater" and "lesser") and by personification (sun to God; moon to humanity). At the heart of this analogy was the assertion that humanity was created in the image of God (1:26–28) for the purpose of "ruling over."

Now, in the pairing of Days 2 and 5, we find evidence to confirm that Day 5 is also built on this same theme of human rulership. In short, Israel was to act as God's appointed rulers by continuing God's control over all the "sea monsters" she would encounter as Joshua led the people into the promised land. However, the book of Joshua gives evidence that Israel was unable to conquer, that is, to rid the "dry" land of Baal worship. Even though Israel was unable to extinguish belief and worship in the gods that populated the minds and beliefs of Canaan's people, nevertheless Israel was expected to subjugate and exercise control over the godless forms of worship by restricting such practices to territories outside of Israel's control. By doing so, the region's gods would be confined and hemmed in between God's convent and Israel's rule. Significantly, Israel was to undertake this charge by working in conjunction with God and not by seeking alliances with foreign rulers.

Leapfrogging into our present era, we find a striking parallel between this ancient creation text and the church's mission today. That connection is bound up in God's commission of rulership. In short, the church is to act as God's appointed ruler to confine—but not eliminate—evil. The church, like Israel, is to continue God's control over all the "sea monsters" which live in the land today. That charge, however, is compromised when it adopts allies from the political world to attain its goals rather than continuing to bond with God's kingdom and Christ's ethically presented message of "good news." The final conquest of evil, that is, its defeat, remains now, as then, in the hands and timing of God's own warrior king, the Lord Almighty,[17] who is shown in the book of Revelation to annihilate evil. Such conquest is affirmed in the prophetic destiny of the race and placed solely in the hands of God. Writing on this topic, Bruce Metzger states:

---

17. See Averbeck, "Ancient Near Eastern Mythography," 354.

God has set a limit to the era of wickedness and will intervene at the appointed time to execute judgment. In the final battle the powers of evil, together with the evil nations they inhabit, will be utterly destroyed. Then a new order will be established, when the End will be as the Beginning, and Paradise will be restored.[18]

SUMMARY

In this chapter, structural focus was on the formula pattern. In it we found seven phrases that were used as a template to shape the story of creation's work. Yet, as noted by Arnold, it was not necessary that each phrase appear in each day's telling. Nevertheless, the omission of some phrases was challenged. We countered with the question that perhaps the absence of a phrase or two was a signal by the author to examine such omissions more closely. That led to the omission of not naming the waters below "seas" and not assessing the work of Day 2 as "good." In these two instances we discovered important links to understand Genesis's theological message. Consequently, turning to Day 3, solutions were discovered.

Significantly, that led to the importance of the non-formula phrase "the dry ground." Through it came understanding that God would not name the sea or call Day 2 "good" until the work of Day 3 was accomplished. In other words, it was only on Day 3 that the submerged land rose out of captivity, having been buried and saturated by the toxic evil of the sea. Thus, the land's rising into view was deemed "good" and, importantly, "dry." With that accomplishment came the climatic conclusion to the *three* days of Panel A. Thus, by the close of those *three* days God had finished his work of making earth—with its *three* environments of sky, land, and sea—into a sacred habitat for the coming of life, depicted in Panel B.

Returning to Days 2 and 5, the phrase "great sea monster" was introduced. Though controversial in the world of biblical translation, use of that designation for the Hebrew word *tanninim* best fits the demands of ancient Israel. With "sea monster" adopted as the best wording, the path to understanding its use was opened. Therefore, the creation narrative's employment of literary structure would be a cause for ancient readers and listeners to notice how *tanninim* was part of a threefold "creation" package in Gen 1. Together, the *threefold* use of the word "creation" formed a literary bracket around the sea monster, and by doing so informed humanity of its

---

18. Metzger, *Breaking the Code*, 24.

God-appointed role, namely, to guard and keep safe the sacred and now-"dry" ground. In the end, we found the presence of the theme of human rulership undergirding each of the three pairs of workdays.

CONCLUSION TO THE TWO-PANEL, THREE-PAIRED WORKDAY STRUCTURE

We noted at the start of this unit how the story of creation was shaped by literary structure, set within a two-panel, three-paired day construction. The very artistry behind the story's formation, therefore, reduced the possibility that Gen 1 was somehow a scientific explanation of how creation came into existence. Rather, literary structure presented a strong argument that Gen 1 was shaped as a mosaic of theological thought.

What was discovered, then, was the biblical theme of human rulership. That interpretation emerged by reading Gen 1 through the two-panel, three-paired day literary structure. Genesis's story of creation, therefore, thematically addresses the rise of human rule, a charge that is fully under the sovereignty of the One Divine Creator.

CHAPTER 5

A Cosmic Temple?

Now that the formerly sea-covered and fully darkened earth has been transformed into a habitat of light and life, the question of purpose is taken up: why did God form the earth into a sacred place? In effect, what was God making as expressed through the artistry of the six-day creation story?

The challenge to understand the creation narrative becomes apparent in Day 7's alteration of the writer's voice. No longer is the proclamation "let there be" heard; instead, we read, "The heavens and the earth were completed." As for content, it is found in the author's announcement "by the seventh day . . . God had finished . . ." Most importantly, though, the standard close-out phrase of the formula pattern, "there was evening, and there was morning the Nth day," is absent. It is replaced with ". . . so on the seventh day he [God] rested from all his work." Not only has the author veered away from formula statements, but he has also reversed creation's content. Elohim is no longer described as creating, making, installing, or separating; now he blesses and sets apart creation's work.

In this chapter, the biblical author's alteration in structure and writing style is investigated. We begin by observing a parallel between Genesis's preface (1:1–2 plus v. 3) and Day 7 (2:1–3), which is considered an epilogue. Next, examination of Day 7 starts with the question of what God made during the six days of creation. This leads to two conclusions. One is a cosmic temple, a term that designates earth to be God's chosen site to meet with humanity. Further, it provides rationale for why God invests humanity with the function of rulership, which is to keep safe God's temple grounds. In the end, we will discover the relationship between this seventh day and Israel's traditions around the Sabbath, which, as a day of cessation from work, is a day set aside to worship the Creator.

A Cosmic Temple?

PREFACE AND EPILOGUE: PARALLELS IN STRUCTURE AND STYLE

A strongly altered written style makes it apparent that in describing Day 7 the biblical author has moved away from the previous pattern found in the six-day sequence. Figure 16 suggests that Day 7 has returned to the format used in the preface of verses 1–3. This is seen by placing the creation story's opening lines and its closing lines into a side-by-side comparison.

FIGURE 16. PREFACE AND EPILOGUE—A COMPARISON

Segments	Preface (1:1–3)	Epilogue (2:1–3)
Opening	"heavens and the earth" (v. 1)	"heavens and the earth" (2:1)
Middle	three-way clause (v. 2)	three-way description (2: 2–3)
Ending	"Let there be light" (v. 3)	"he (Elohim) rested" (2:3)

To comprehend this more clearly, the epilogue is quoted below. The NRSVUE is employed since it more accurately lists the word "God" three times in comparison to the NIV's twice employment.[1] Use of the word "God" three times (emphasis added in quote below) brings focus upon God, who on the seventh day is found to (1) have finished creation's work, (2) blessed and hallowed it, and (3) rested (i.e., ceased) from all his work. Of the seventh day, the writer proclaims:

> Thus the heavens and the earth were finished and all their multitude. On the sixth day *God* finished the work that he had done, and he rested on the seventh day from all the work that he had done. So *God* blessed the seventh day and hallowed it, because on it *God* rested from all the work that he had done in creation. (Gen 2:1–2)

Noteworthy in this text is the implied question, What was God doing? That thought emerges directly from the text, which states, "God had finished the work he had been doing." Thus, we must ask, what was the aim of Elohim's creation activity?

---

1. See NET, note "g," Gen 2:3.

BEYOND MYTH

WHAT GOD MADE: A COSMIC TEMPLE?

FIGURE 17. OVERALL STRUCTURE OF THE CREATION WEEK

Segment	Location		
Preface	1:1-2 + v. 3: The story of creation unfolds		
Main Body (days 1-6)	Panel 'A'		Panel 'B'
	Day 1	→	Day 4
	Day 2	→	Day 5
	Day 3	→	Day 6
Epilogue	2:1-3: The story of creation concludes (i.e., Day 7)		

Figure 17 shows that the story of creation is told in three parts: the preface (its opening), the main body of content (its middle), and the epilogue (its ending). In our examination of Gen 1's main body, the six days of God's work, we discovered how the author depicted that work through symmetrical correspondences. In Panel A, God transformed the primordial sea from a place of darkness and disorder (and in the minds of the ancient world one in which mythic gods dwelt) to one of light and stated goodness. This resulted in the earth becoming a sacred site, affirmed through the *sevenfold* use of the word "good" with emphasis on "the dry ground." Hence, the earth was made into a suitable site in which the Creator King would meet with his primary life form, humanity.

Of that, Meredith Kline puts it this way.

> Another [literary] architectural dimension of creation comes to view in the course of biblical revelation. Creation was designed to serve a far more exalted function than the housing of a variety of creature-beings in the distinctive areas of the earth. The cosmic structure was built as a habitation for the Creator himself. Heaven and earth were erected as a house of God, a palace of the Great King, the seat of sovereignty of the Lord of the covenant."[2]

In this quote, Kline moves from the function of creation—which was to bring order and life—to stating God's purpose in creation. Thus, he refers to a "cosmic structure." In other words, what we may think of as a temple. In the ancient world, earthly temples were the designated meeting places

2. Kline, *Kingdom Prologue*, 27.

between the gods and humankind. T. Desmond Alexander, referencing John Walton, writes on this temple theme:

> He [Walton] observes that in extrabiblical accounts [such as epic poems of the ancient Near East] when gods become involved in creative activity, they do so to make for themselves a resting place. Normally this involves the creation of a temple that stands at the heart of a city. Divine rest is associated with temple building.[3]

J. R. Middleton, having reviewed the creation sequence, affirms this conclusion. "The text, then, by its careful literary artistry, evokes a creator-God carefully constructing an artful world according to a well-thought-out plan for the benefit of creatures."[4] Continuing, he asks, "But we may inquire further into just *what* the divine designer and artisan is making in Genesis 1?"[5] After surveying several Old Testament passages, Middleton concludes, "God is building a temple."[6]

T. Desmond Alexander further supports this as he writes, "Interpreted against their ancient Near Eastern background, the opening chapters of Genesis anticipate that God's plans for the earth center on the creation of an extraordinary temple-city where God will dwell in harmony with humanity."[7] Thus, Alexander sees the creation text pointing to God's work to form earth into a sacred temple-city in which God and humanity may dwell together, forever living in sacred unity.

Tabernacle/Temple Through Structure and Style

The author of the New Testament's letter to the Hebrews considers God's instruction to Moses to build a tabernacle so profoundly important that he inserted it into his correspondence. "They [i.e., priests] offer worship in a sanctuary that is a sketch and shadow of the heavenly one; for Moses, when he was about to erect the tent [i.e., tabernacle], was warned, 'See that you make everything according to the pattern that was shown you on the mountain'" (Heb 8:5, based on Exod 25:40).

---

3. Alexander, *Paradise*, 123. (PhD, Queen's University, Belfast; Director of Postgraduate Studies, Senior Lecturer in Biblical Studies, Union Theological College.)
4. Middleton, *Liberating Image*, 77.
5. Middleton, *Liberating Image*, 77.
6. Middleton, *Liberating Image*, 81.
7. Alexander, *Paradise*, 119.

Here, the Hebrew author is writing out of the mindset of the ancient world. Of that, Bernhard Anderson wrote, "Ancient man believed that the ordered structure of the universe—heaven, earth, and underearth—was evident in the fact that things terrestrial are replicas or copies of their heavenly prototypes. The temple on earth, for instance, was thought to be a copy of the deity's heavenly Temple . . ."[8]

The tabernacle, through its physical layout, projects a visual image. It faithfully represents the "pattern that was shown you on the mountain." The tabernacle itself was triadic in structure: it had a courtyard, and inside was a two-parted tent. One part was referred to as "the holy place." The other, and innermost, bore the title "the most holy place" (or holy of holies). In the holy place were three objects: an incense altar, the table of showcase (with the bread of presence), and a golden lamp stand. The lamp stand was one piece in construction. It was formed by one central pole which held two branches of three arms on either side. Once inside the innermost part, that is the holy of holies, was found one object, the ark of the covenant. The ark contained three objects: the tablets given to Moses, manna retained from the forty years of wilderness wandering, and Aaron's rod, which had budded. The entire complex was aligned on a west-to-east trajectory facing the sunrise (i.e., "the greater light"), which represented God's splendor (Hab 3:4).[9]

The above description demonstrates how Israel's tabernacle—which was copied over from the pattern of the heavenly template—was based on the number *three*. It is not difficult to perceive in this numerical correspondence a distinct harmony between Moses' instructions to build a tabernacle and the architectural design of the creation story. After all, earth's three life zones—sky, land, sea—reflect a sacred yet *triadic* outline. When biblical scholars speak of God constructing a temple and the writer of Hebrews reports Israel's tabernacle is based on a heavenly pattern, what readily comes into sight is creation as a cosmic temple.

Further, by recalling scholars who stress the importance of biblical structure to story meaning, an architectural correspondence can be drawn. It is clear the number *three* underlies the creation narrative. It is also evident, as the writer to Hebrews makes known, Moses was commanded to build a tabernacle (i.e., forerunner to the temple) according to the heavenly

---

8. Anderson, *Creation Versus Chaos*, 116. (PhD, Yale University; Professor Emeritus in Old Testament Theology, Princeton University.)

9. See *Rose Book of Bible Charts*, 146–47.

A Cosmic Temple?

pattern. Thus, the building of the tabernacle and the creation story find correspondence in the architectural foundation of *three*. This relationship is depicted in figure 18.

Figure 18. Story Structure and Temple Construction

Structure of creation days		Structure of tabernacle	
Days 1–3	Days 4–6	The holy place	Holy of holies
Day 7		Outer courtyard	

Figure 18 can be read in two dimensions. The first is the outline shape of the seven-day creation narrative, a story told in *three* parts: (a) Days 1–3, (b) Days 4–6, and (c) Day 7. But this same story-shape also outlines the geometry of the tabernacle/temple, which too is built on a *threefold* pattern (courtyard, holy place, holy of holies). Hence, the form of the tabernacle tent echoes the literary form of the creation story. Both are based on the biblical cadence of *three*. John Walton and other scholars build a case for the symbolism of the temple and the garden of Eden. Walton writes, "If Eden is the center of sacred space, it bears some resemblance to the holies of holies in the tabernacle/temple."[10]

Christian Eberhart writes, "The design, function, and purpose of altars and sanctuaries mentioned in the Hebrew Bible are by no means unique . . ."[11] He continues, "Israel's sacred sites and sanctuaries conform more or less to the design and purpose of the sanctuaries of these surrounding cultures."[12] Another way to say that is the biblical creation story adheres to regional myths in which the gods, at the conclusion of creation, engaged in temple-building. Such correspondences are easily understood in the mathematical and visual connections described above, as well as the floral decor adorning walls and doors of Israel's temple (see, for example, 1 Kgs 6:18, 29, 32, 35). Desmond Alexander notes, "This explains why many of the decorative features of the tabernacle and temple are arboreal in nature."[13]

Scholars believe that Israel's tabernacle and the lushness of the garden, alongside the cultural myths of the ancient Near East, depict Elohim

---

10. Walton, *Lost World of Adam and Eve*, 117.

11. Eberhart, *Sacrifice of Jesus*, 34. (Double PhD; Professor of Religious Studies and Comparative Cultural Studies, University of Houston.)

12. Eberhart, *Sacrifice of Jesus*, 34.

13. Alexander, *Eden*, 25.

at work building a cosmic temple. Therefore, we find in favor of those who conclude that the symmetrical description of creation through triads (i.e., the three paired days) is in fact the story of God preparing earth to be a temple on a grand, even a "cosmic" scale. Alexander adds to this theme, writing of Genesis's earliest audiences, "They would have quickly realized that Eden was the greenfield site designated by God to be the location for his temple-city."[14]

SUMMARY

This chapter began with the question, What was God building in the creation narrative? By reviewing literary structure, consulting Bible scholars, layering upon this the cultural context of the ancient Near East; by observing the heavenly pattern on which the tabernacle was built; by remembering that Genesis holds ancient Israel's shaped memories and traditions, all leads to one conclusive thought: God's work of creation is a work to bring heaven, which is "above," down to earth, which is "below." That geocentric sight line joins God's sacred realm above with terrestrial earth, humanity's home, and so the Genesis storyteller writes, "Thus the heavens and the earth were completed." This joining together is the intent of the *imago Dei*—that is, the "image of God"—in whose likeness humanity is created. The formation of the garden temple is a sacred work; it sanctifies and makes holy the ground on which humanity lives and has its dwelling. In that, the "dry ground" out of which humanity was formed (2:7) echoes the joined togetherness of mankind and the sacred, all of which reveals the motivation behind the creation of humanity: vice-rulership and worship.

CHAPTER CONCLUSION

It is evident, therefore, that the "rest" described in the sacred seventh day fulfills God's intent at the outset of creation as he separates "the light" from "the darkness" (1:2). In that regard, the preface of 1:1–2, plus verse 3, reminds ancient readers of what they know: the creation story is being told from the lens of Israel's traditions, of which the separation of "the light" from "the darkness" are contrasting counterparts. The "light" of Day 1 is not part of the universe's natural order. It stands apart. Similarly, the "rest"

---

14. Alexander, *Paradise*, 126.

A Cosmic Temple?

of Day 7 is not part of the universe's natural rhythms in which animals and humanity periodically repose. Rather, the "rest" of the seventh day is perpetual, much as the "light" from Day 1 is constant and always. Genesis, as a creation story, marks "the beginning," that is, the starting point of Yahweh's desire to invite humanity into an eternal, perpetual, and never-ending relationship, one that is hallmarked with forever light and constant love. These are the ingredients of God's rest, a framework for human worship.

It appears, therefore, that what God made through creation was the transformation of earth into a holy dwelling place in which he may reside with humanity. We see glimpses of that in the paradise garden as God walks with the man in the cool of the day (3:8). T. Desmond Alexander writes, "God intends that the world should become his dwelling place."[15] In the ancient world, priests served in temples built to house various gods. When readers come to Gen 2, the text declares, "The Lord God took the man and put him in the Garden in Eden to work it and take care of it." The phrase "to work and take care of" alludes to the duties and tasks of Israel's priesthood. John Walton puts it this way: "The terms 'serve' [i.e., the NIV's "work"] and 'keep' [i.e., the NIV's "take care"] convey priestly tasks rather than landscaping and agrarian responsibilities."[16] Later Walton clarifies this role, writing of priests in the ancient world, "The main task of the priest was the preservation of sacred space."[17]

By combining the priestly role designated to Adam and Eve with the sacred image imprinted on them by virtue of being made in God's likeness, the Genesis writer foresees *a royal role for humanity*. The race is to prepare the way for the heavenly visitation of the Creator King. In the race's commissioning, two duties are prescribed. One is protective; the human couple must keep the garden safe as a sacred space. As for the second, the purpose of humanity is to worship *El Shaddai* (Hebrew for "God Almighty").

Of the former thought—"protect the sacred"—much will be said when we enter directly into the garden in Gen 3. Worship, on the other hand, is the direct outcome of the sacred *seventh* day. That would have been easily understood by ancient Israel, being ratified through the nation's most sacred document, which was given out of the hands of God and placed into the arms of Moses.

---

15. Alexander, *Eden*, 26.
16. Walton, *Lost World of Adam and Eve*, 105.
17. Walton, *Lost World of Adam and Eve*, 108.

Beyond Myth

> Remember the Sabbath day by keeping it holy.
> Six days you shall labor and do all your work,
> but the seventh day is a sabbath to the Lord your God (Exod 20:8).

Hence, the "Sabbath rest" of the Ten Commandments becomes the clarion call to the nation: Israel is to be a worshiping community. Bernhard Anderson writes, "The creation story is most at home in a setting of worship."[18] Jon Levenson picks up this theme in chapter 8 of his book, writing, "The Priestly theology of creation is inextricably associated with the observance of the Sabbath."[19]

UNIT CONCLUSION

Unit 1 was based on the following concepts, keys for understanding Gen 1–11.

- Genesis is an ancient text.
- The creation narrative is the story of ancient Israel, her beginnings as a faith community, and, most importantly, it is God's story.
- The text itself is not written in the language of science nor the ways of modern history writing.
- Interpretive keys, common to the ancient world, need to be accessed to authentically interpret and discern the author's message. Three keys are literary structure, author style, and ancient culture. These interpretive keys will be employed throughout the duration of this two-volume series.
- Biblical numbers are emerging as a platform for scriptural understanding.
- The narrative is centered on God, the majestic Elohim, creator of the heavens and earth, and by extrapolation consistent with today's knowledge of science, the creator of the universe.
- Elohim is the text's chief character, and though not always in sight, nevertheless his presence is what gives meaning to creation's story.
- Importantly, the text declares that humanity is created in God's image, which equates to rulership in conjunction with the Divine Creator.

---

18. Anderson, *Creation Versus Chaos*, 83.
19. Levenson, *Persistence of Evil*, 100.

A Cosmic Temple?

That creation text (Gen 1:27) commences the rise of human rule in the biblical narrative.

- Human rule cannot be separated from human priesthood; thus, humans are formed in God's image, caretakers of scared space, and vested with a worship impulse that is satisfied when devotion is given to the Divine Creator.
- God's ambition, as expressed through ancient Israel's creation-faith, is to take up residence on the earth and dwell within it as a holy and blessed "cosmic temple."
- The theme of light and darkness is evident at this point, as is the biblical theme of human rulership under God's oversight.
- For the church today, elements of a "plumb line" are being assembled, some of which are goodness, integrity, harmony, sacredness, joining in allegiance with the Divine Creator and him only, and worshipful living. These are some of the standards by which human rulership and the church's missional charge may be assessed. Further, this commission is activated through the confinement of darkness and not by the church's joining with those who seek their own glory, power, and greatness.

UNIT 2

Garden

IN THE PREVIOUS UNIT, we found God at work transforming an already existent earth (the primordial sea) into a sacred site where he might meet with the pride of creation, humanity. Transitioning to Unit 2, we come upon Eden, and within it is found a special garden, a "cosmic temple" site. What happens there is the story of Unit 2.

This unit takes up a second creation narrative, which is largely set in the paradise garden. It offers a contrast to that presented in Genesis chapter 1. We find in Gen 2, therefore, a story considerably different in content but not purpose. However, before we move too deeply into the garden, we will first pause to gain understanding of certain essential words which function as images, such as "tree," "marriage," and "serpent." With that ancient background in mind, the events in the garden can be more thoughtfully examined. Those events are often seen as the "fall" of man, being laced with verbiage transported over from other biblical contexts and traditions, such as "sin," "transgression," and "rebellion." But is that what Gen 2 and 3 teach? Yet, despite the importance of those questions, what we wonder most is how this unit presents the theme of human rulership.

CHAPTER 6

Structure in the Second Creation Story

To transition from Gen 1 to Gen 2, we begin with a story retell. Our purpose is to draw a comparison between Genesis's two opening chapters by familiarizing ourselves with the content of the second story.

THE ACCOUNT OF GEN 2: A STORY RETELL

As we engage chapter 2 of Genesis, we find the story of creation altered and the Creator, whom we knew as Elohim in chapter 1, has a new name...

> Yahweh is present. He is not far removed as might be some god of the ancient Near East who, having established the heavens and the earth, now retreats to loiter around a faraway galaxy. Rather, we find Yahweh near, having staked out a section of the earth in which he has planted a garden. Into it he places the man he has formed out of earth's dust and having breathed into his nostrils the "breath of life," this *man* has become a "living being" (2:7). It is there, in that garden, Yahweh gives the man certain instructions, issuing him a kind of verbal survival manual. The man is to avoid at all costs eating fruit from a banned tree referred to as "the tree of the knowledge of good and evil" (2:9).
>
> Though the man is enthralled by the garden's beauty, it seems that all is not "good" (contrary to what we might expect given the first creation story's emphasis on that word). Yahweh takes notice of the man's unhappy plight: "It is not good for the man to be alone" (2:18). He endeavors to rectify this blemish by bringing to the man all the animals of the field and birds of the sky. Momentarily this works; the man busily names each kind. Yet, when the procession

is over the man is still without a "suitable helper." Yahweh moves to rectify that condition. Yahweh anesthetizes the man and lifts a rib from his side and, as a potter might, fashions it into a like being. As the man awakens and sights this *new "adam"* (i.e., "human") he is enraptured. She is indeed made in his likeness, but in certain essential ways, ways which delight the man, she is different. Their nakedness, which is no cause for shame, they soon learn to enjoy.

COMPARING GEN 2 TO GEN 1: STORY QUESTIONS

Several questions quickly confront us in Gen 2. We wonder where this new story of creation ends. Another question is, Why has the biblical author renamed Elohim? Now he is Yahweh (Hebrew "LORD"). Further, our reflection is filled with mythological images. We find "the man" being made of the earth's dust, and regarding the land, Yahweh has planted a garden into which he puts the man. This garden holds special trees; there is a tree of life—but also a tree of the knowledge of good and evil. Then there is an animal parade, all brought before the man in search of a suitable helpmate. Clearly this story of creation is completely different than the stately sequence of creation's six days.

Indeed, Gen 1 and 2 are presented with distinctly different events. Such content changes convince many that these chapters are two unique accounts and not just one larger story broken into two halves. In this manuscript, reference is made to creation as stories (plural). This is likely unsettling, even controversial for many readers. This is done, however, not regarding the question of how many authors wrote these two creation accounts, which by tradition is one—Moses—or since the nineteenth century's *documentary hypothesis*, two.[1]

---

1. The documentary hypothesis is a theological framework. It postulates the origin and composition of the Pentateuch, the first five books of the Bible. The German biblical scholar Julius Wellhausen is credited with its popularization in the late nineteenth century. Over time, it came to be modified in a variety of ways. Its reception into current academia is similarly varied. Presently it is rejected by most conservative Christian scholars. Its basic tenet holds that four sources were responsible for the composition of the Jewish Torah. While conservatives remain strongly fixed on Moses as the one (or main author), the hypothesis affirms authorship by at least four writers, known as J, E, P, and D. (A helpful review of the documentary hypothesis is given by T. Desmond Alexander in *From Paradise to the Promised Land*; see his chapter 4.) For a conceptual look at the biblical writers known as P and J, purported to have authored Gen 1 (P) and Gen 2 (J), see Anderson, p. 58 and all of chapter 2 in *Creation Versus Chaos*. Anderson connects

Structure in the Second Creation Story

Reference, then, to two stories is based on a comparison of content, how each one tells a singularly different version of creation. Indeed, Umberto Cassuto finds that the second story is not so much creation at all. He argues that the creation composition arose out of two traditions: "The one dealing with the story of creation and the other with that of the garden of Eden, were of different types."[2] Peter Bouteneff writes of a "clear division" between the first creation story (1:1–2:4a) and the second (2:4b-3:24), stating, "I speak of the creation *narratives* in the plural."[3] He adds, "Far from a redundant retelling, then, the two accounts fulfill different functions and are, for the purposes of subsequent thinking, both indispensable."[4]

Joseph Blenkinsopp nicely summarizes the debate over one or two creation stories. He writes, "The perspective now [Gen 2] is local rather than cosmic [Gen 1]. Instead of a shapeless mass, darkness and a great wind (Gen. 1:1–2), there is an earth without vegetation and inhabitants (2:5)."[5] Blenkinsopp points to vocabulary differences, such as the Hebrew word *asah* ("makes") rather than *bara* ("creates"). He notes in the making of man that his formation is described as a potter might work clay. Further, Blenkinsopp cites a garden, the process of anesthetizing the man coupled with the female's formation, and how God talks to the two humans. He concludes, "Hence, this second story about origins has practically nothing in common with the one preceding it and nowhere refers to it. The juxtaposition of the two narratives nevertheless challenges the reader to look for connections..."[6]

By building on Blenkinsopp and others, particularly Robert Graves and Raphael Patai, a table comparing the two Genesis creation stories emerges, illustrated in figure 19.

---

the documentary hypothesis's four writers with Israel's geographical history. Hence, J and P are associated with the Southern Kingdom, while the traditions of E and D are ascribed to the Northern Kingdom. Anderson's portrayal of these "two streams" (north and south), though written over a half century ago, continues to be a relevant text.

2. Cassuto, *Commentary on Genesis*, 72.
3. Bouteneff, *Beginnings*, 2.
4. Bouteneff, *Beginnings*, 3.
5. Blenkinsopp, *Creation, Un-creation, Re-creation*, 54. (PhD, University of Oxford; John A. O'Brien Professor of Biblical Studies, University of Notre Dame).
6. Blenkinsopp, *Creation, Un-creation, Re-creation*, 54.

Beyond Myth

Figure 19. Comparison: Chapter 1 to 2[7]

Gen 1	Gen 2
Elohim (God) created all, the universe and everything in it, including earth, which was formless, empty, and dark.	Yahweh (the LORD God) made earth and the heavens.
• Light	• A mist (or streams) watered the ground
• Firmament (sky)	• Unnamed man formed
• Dry land emerges	• Yahweh plants a garden
• Grass and trees	• Man placed into the garden
• Solar lights	• Two special trees are highlighted
• Sea life	• Geographical locations cited
• Sky life	• Animals and birds are formed
• Land life	• Woman is formed
• Human life (man and woman in his image)	

Plainly, these two stories are related but not replications; they are more like cousins than brothers and sisters having the same parents. They contain what some call contradictions or dichotomies, seen for example in the alteration of story sequence, such as the second story, in which the man is formed prior to all other life, while the woman's advent is delayed until after the animals have been formed. Brayford writes of sequential contrasts, noting, "The second account goes back to a time before the greening of the fields of the earth."[8] If readers who have never read these two biblical stories were asked to read them for the first time, undoubtedly they would find them more different than alike, that is, two stories rather than one broken into two parts. Yet, in opposition to such a conclusion, C. John Collins hypothesizes that the events of story two fall within the sixth day, thus making the second story a kind of expanded flashback. He argues, "But Genesis 1:27 takes place on day 6 of the creation week; this would mean that 2:7–25 does as well."[9] He is not alone in this view. But is that possible?

The purpose of this chapter is to give an overview of Gen 2 by comparing it to Gen 1, which was completed in the above description. Next, an examination of structure, in which the "*toledot* phrase" is featured, picks

7. Figure 19 was built on information from Graves, *Hebrew Myths*, 21–24.
8. Brayford, *Genesis*, 227.
9. Collins, *Genesis 1–4*, 110.

Structure in the Second Creation Story

up the importance of literary structure in Genesis. No longer is the biblical author asserting a "formula pattern," nor is he employing a two-panel structure to inform meaning.

STRUCTURE IN GEN 2

At this point there is need to introduce the term "*toledot* phrase." *Toledot* is a Hebrew word that means "generations" or "descendants." At times it is translated the "family histories of..." Its importance to our study is found in its recurrence throughout the book of Genesis. Figure 20 displays its usage in Gen 1–11. As a clause it may be read, "This is the account of..." or "These are the generations of..."[10] This clause is first encountered in Gen 2:4, and thereafter it signals start and stop points for Genesis's several units. Figure 20 identifies *toledot* placements in the first eleven chapters. The *toledot* phrase is not limited to Gen 1–11 but may be found in Gen 12–50 as well. For that reason, many consider it the primary organizational structure of this book. As such, it answers the question of Unit 2's ending point, which comes at Gen 4:26.

Figure 20. Toledot Phrases in Gen 1–11

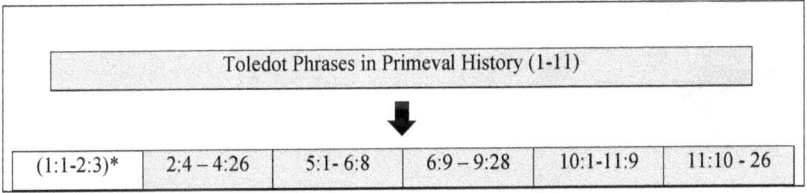

* The first unit does not start with this clause.

Building on this construction, figure 21 sketches the structure of the second unit, which is referred to as *the second creation narrative*. It is set upon three interconnected stories. In this book, unit stories are referred to as *passages*; thus the first passage in this unit is "The Man and the Woman." That passage is broken into three parts, called segments. These are formed by verses (a) 5–7, (b) 8–17, and (c) 18–25. To be sure, not all scholars agree with this threefold structure. For example, C. John Collins finds four divisions (vv. 5–9, 10–14, 15–17, and 18–25).[11] Victor Hamilton uses vv. 4–7,

10. See NET, Translator note "i," Gen 2:4.
11. Collins, *Genesis 1–4*, 103.

8–9, 10–14, 15–17, 18–20, 21–25 for his analysis.[12] Somewhat different is Umberto Cassuto, who sees the chapter composed of four paragraphs (vv. 5–7, 8–13, 15–17, 18–25), while Kenneth Matthews outlines the passage in three segments (vv. 4–7, 8–17, and 18–25[13]), as presented in figure 21. Regardless, most would find the formation of the woman as the passage's position of prominence, that is, its climatic peak. To illustrate, Collins writes of the final two verses (i.e., 23–24), they "are the peak of the pericope" (i.e., the passage).[14]

Before examining this passage, we need to hear from David Dorsey. He is known for his work in Old Testament literary structure. Dorsey points to how biblical authorship "utilized *positions of prominence* to reinforce or convey meaning (emphasis added)."[15]

FIGURE 21. LITERARY STRUCTURE IN UNIT 2

Unit	Unit Title	Passages in Unit 2	Passage Segments
2:4 – 4:26	The Second Creation Narrative (2:4-4:26)	The Man and the Woman (2:4-25)	Vss. 5-7
			Vss. 8-17
			Vss. 18-25
		Into the Garden (3:1-24)	*(Examined later)*
		East of Eden (4:1-26)	*(Examined in Volume Two)*

In today's literary world it is standard practice for authors to locate a story's conclusion, that is the plot's climax, at the end of a tale. But in Hebrew writing that was not always the case. Dorsey describes several literary structures common to the Old Testament. In one, referred to as symmetrical, the climax occurs in the middle, not the end, whereas another, referred to as linear, places the climax at the end. Over the course of this unit, we will encounter both. For now, we introduce linear structure as most commentators work from that view (figure 22).

12. Hamilton, *Book of Genesis*, 150, 160, 166, 171, 174, 177.
13. Matthews, *Genesis 1–11:26*, 183.
14. Collins, *Genesis 1-4*, 133.
15. Dorsey, *Literary Structure*, 39.

Structure in the Second Creation Story

Figure 22. Genesis 2 and Linear Structure

1st Segment	2nd Segment	3rd Segment
(vss. 4b-7)	(vss. 8-17)	(vss. 18-25)
Forming the man from out of the ground	Garden – land and covenant	Making the woman from out of the man

Linear Development and Passage Climax

Figure 22 displays this passage as being developed in three scenes (segments). In the first, the man is formed out of the ground. In the next, God's covenant for living within the garden of Eden is detailed. That gives way to the passage's essential question, What will God do to resolve the man's loneliness (v. 18)? That is answered in the formation of the woman, who is made from the man's rib, or side. Thus, this episode rises to its climax with the making of the woman in the final segment. Hence, Dorsey's "position of prominence" can be located here at the end of this linear progression. Strangely, it is also here that the biblical storyteller suddenly inserts a picture of marriage, seen by portraying the woman as "wife." The text states, "That is why a man leaves his father and mother and is united to his wife, and they become one flesh" (2:24).

SUMMARY

In this short chapter both Unit 2 and Gen 2 were introduced; emphasis was on comparing Gen 1 to Gen 2. Doing so we found that these two creation accounts were more different than similar. Enough so, like many scholars, we conclude they are two different stories and not just one which might somehow be combined, such as Collins proposes by reading Gen 2 as a flashback to creation's Day 6.

Second, this chapter introduced Genesis's literary structure from three points of view. The first answered the question, What is the overall structure of Gen 1–11? By use of the "*toledot* phrase," we saw how Genesis's eleven chapters formed six units (see figure 20). Next, we looked at the second unit's overall structure. We found it to be constructed in three passages (figure 21), which ran from Gen 2 to Gen 4. Moving on to the chapter level, we found Gen 2 comprised of a threefold schematic, displayed in figure 22. Additionally, we learned that this chapter was built on a linear model. This is like modern-day literature in which a story's climax is located at a book's end. In this case, that ending entailed the formation of the woman, climaxing as the biblical author used the words "wife," "naked," and "not ashamed." How that plays out will be seen in the following chapters, which continues this look at structure and meaning.

CHAPTER 7

Symmetry in the Second Creation Story

GENESIS 2, COMING AS it does between chapters 1 and 3, links the first story of creation to the events in the paradise garden. Figures 23 and 24 reveal that this linkage occurs in the literary use of symmetry.

FIGURE 23: SYMMETRY IN THE CREATION STORY

	Symmetry In Gen 1 and Gen 2		
Text 1:26	Gen 1 Let us make mankind in our image, in our likeness, so that they may rule over	Gen 2 The Lord God took the man and put him in the Garden of Eden to work it and take care of it.	Text 2:15

R. W. L. Moberly remarks on this connection. "YHWH'S setting the human in the garden with responsibility over it (2:15) is conceptually similar to God's gift of dominion [i.e. rulership] over creation (1:26-28) . . ." Figure 23 displays Moberly's observation, in which the relationship between human rulership and garden oversight ("work and take care," which are temple duties performed by Israel's priests) points to how the biblical author is using symmetry to inform his message.

Figure 24 discloses additional and like detail. This can be seen in the parallel structuring of the text. Here, in verse 4a and 4b, the symmetry of the heavens and earth not only closes the first creation account (2:4a) but begins the second (2:4b). And then again, this same pattern is found in verse 8a and 8b in which God plants a garden and places within it the man. Surely, this artful depiction is intentional and not accidental. Not only is the biblical author relocating the story from the heavenlies (i.e., "creation above") to the terrestrial sphere (i.e., the "garden" below), but he is structurally shaping the second story through symmetry. Thus, the creation story of Gen 1 shifts from the "heavens" to the earth/garden below in Gen 2.

FIGURE 24: SHAPING THE TEXT THROUGH SYMMETRY

Symmetry In Gen 2			
Text 2:4a 2:4b	Creation heavens and the earth the earth and the heavens	Garden planted a garden put the man	Text 2:8a 2:8b

These illustrations reveal how the biblical author made use of symmetry to enhance his writing. The purpose of this chapter, therefore, is to identify symmetry as an important part of literary structure and determine how the biblical author used it to further story meaning.

HEBREW STRUCTURE

David Dorsey wrote, "All literary compositions have structure."[1] Applying that to the Old Testament, Dorsey wrote of common difficulties when analyzing biblical structure. One is a lack of "graphic structure markers to help readers follow"[2] a document. Here, he means that ancient texts were not written using common conventions known to us today, such as paragraph structure, since texts ran on and on continuously. In Israel's ancient scrolls, there were no organization aids, such as chapters and verses or spacing between major thought-breaks. Dorsey describes the difficulty of reading a text "without set-off titles, subtitles, indentations, or other visual structure indicators."[3] In other words, ancient texts were totally unlike modern publications that hold a variety of features, all intended to guide readers to understand an author's message.

1. Dorsey, *Literary Structure*, 15.
2. Dorsey, *Literary Structure*, 15.
3. Dorsey, *Literary Structure*, 15.

Symmetry in the Second Creation Story

Nevertheless, the ancients were not without structural assistance. Mostly though, that help came in auditory form, since readers of ancient texts were mainly hearers of it. "An ancient writer was compelled to use structural signals that would be perceptible to the listening audience. Signals were geared for the ear; not the eye."[4] This need, driven by the ear and not the eye, resulted in the development of a variety of features for the listener. Among them, as Dorsey continues, were "symmetry, parallelism, and structured repetition."[5]

Thus, the biblical author's purpose for investing writing with literary structure is to provide guidance to a text's listeners, signals that direct understanding as Scripture is read. Hence, Dorsey lays out the case of structure's importance, noting that the "task in studying the structure of an Old Testament book is to consider the relationship of the book's structure to its meaning."[6] Three broad ways structure conveyed meaning to a listener may be found in: "(1) the composition's overall structure, (2) [its] structured repetition, and (3) positions of prominence."[7]

When Dorsey wrote of "positions of prominence" to spotlight meaning, he is thinking of how a biblical author intentionally positioned within a text its high point. He clarifies, "Hebrew literary tradition also had standard positions of prominence for various structural schemes."[8] Among those schemes were linear and symmetrical constructions. Hence, "the position of prominence in linear and parallel schemes, for example, is generally the final unit"[9] (i.e., the end of a book or passage). In contrast, when a passage is built on symmetry, "The center [i.e., the "peak"] is normally the natural position of prominence."[10] Dorsey quotes three scholars who define the term "position of prominence." They wrote, "Prominence is simply making one or more parts of a unit [i.e., such as a passage] more important than the other parts."[11]

Returning to symmetry, Dorsey adds, "When the *symmetry has an odd number* of units the central unit is further accented because it is the

---

4. Dorsey, *Literary Structure*, 16.
5. Dorsey, *Literary Structure*, 16.
6. Dorsey, *Literary Structure*, 36.
7. Dorsey, *Literary Structure*, 36.
8. Dorsey, *Literary Structure*, 40.
9. Dorsey, *Literary Structure*, 40.
10. Dorsey, *Literary Structure*, 40.
11. Dorsey, *Literary Structure*, 39n8.

only unmatched unit" (emphasis added).[12] This often leads to symmetrical passages being built around comparison and contrast. Hence, when a passage has an odd number of segments, its climax is located at its *center* rather than, as is normal in written communication today, its conclusion. How this important concept looks is now taken up.

SYMMETRICAL STRUCTURE IN GEN 2

Genesis 2, in addition to having a linear structure, can also be seen as symmetrically formed. In the case of Gen 2, symmetry is built on comparison, that of the man in contrast to the woman. This symmetrical comparison leaves the passage's high point centered in God's covenant issuance. This view, therefore, transforms the linear and rectangularly shaped structure, which was presented in chapter 6, into one that can be visualized triangularly, seen in figure 25. It is here that Dorsey's reference to symmetrical and positions of prominence comes into play.

Figure 25 projects Gen 2 as symmetrically constructed. In this odd-numbered passage (comprising the three segments identified as A, A', and B), symmetry occurs through a comparison of the two humans. Namely, the man's formation (segment A) out of clay lies in sharp contrast to the woman's making (segment A'), which occurs from out of the man's rib (or side). But this view of structure, unlike linear construction, does not find the high point occurring with the woman's making. Instead, through symmetrical structure, passage peak comes in the center (segment B).

FIGURE 25. SYMMETRICAL STRUCTURE IN GEN 2

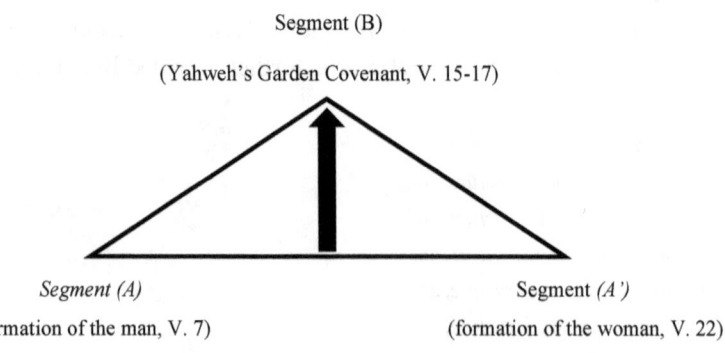

12. Dorsey, *Literary Structure*, 40.

Symmetry in the Second Creation Story

It is from this intentionally centered position of prominence that God issues a declaration describing the conditions of conduct expected of those who live in the garden. What this alteration of prominence means—from story endpoint to story middle—is that the narrative flow is no longer linear. Rather, the thrust of the passage occurs as God speaks to the man. In other words, the author's interest lies in a theological pronouncement and not a scientific description.

To restate this, the most prominent moment in Gen 2 is the description of God giving *adam*/human various instructions on how to live in the garden. With that in mind, we will now examine Genesis 2 by starting at the passage's high point: God's proclamation to the man (at this point the woman has yet to be formed).

Covenant—Passage Peak

In the middle segment (vv. 8–17), primary emphasis comes at verses 15 through 17. There Yahweh issues a covenant to the man. A biblical covenant occurs at God's initiative. In this case, God lays out the conditions for how the man (and the woman yet to be formed) may live in relationship to him in the paradise garden. However, because the word "covenant" is not found in this passage, not all recognize that this is what the text is describing.

Here, Collins is helpful. "Some theologians have called God's arrangement with Adam (Gen. 2:15–17) a covenant."[13] Collins provides rationale for this conclusion, writing, "It [covenant] comes from God's initiative; verses 16–17 clearly spell out the condition for the man, namely, obedience to God's command."[14] We find this as Yahweh exhorts, "You are free to eat from any tree in the garden; but you must not eat from the tree of the knowledge of good and evil, for when you eat from it you will certainly die" (2:16–17). Thomas Schreiner comes close to labeling this a covenant, implying such as he writes of God's stipulation, "The call to obedience forecasts the Mosaic covenant . . ."[15] But it is the work of Meredith Kline that most convincingly identifies 2:16–17 as a covenant.. He states, "Certainly the substance of *berith* [Hebrew for covenant] was present in the kingdom

---

13. Collins, *Genesis 1–4*, 112.
14. Collins, *Genesis 1–4*, 113.
15. Schreiner, *King in His Beauty*, 8.

order described in Genesis 1–3. It was characterized by precisely those elements that constitute a covenant . . ."[16]

Kline's statement likely causes problems for readers who think of covenant as involving an animal sacrifice to institute it, such as in Gen 15. There, verse 18 reads, "On that day the LORD made a covenant with Abram . . ." which was instituted through the sacrifice of "a heifer, a goat, and a ram" (v. 9). But more so, this covenant promise was symbolized by reference to the uncountable stars in the heavens, thus representing God's faithfulness to form a nation out of Abram (v. 5). In Gen 17, the text reaffirms this with the promise of land (Canaan, v. 8). Here, the yet-to-be-given land becomes a sign of covenant fulfillment, though it would not take place until well after Abraham's death. The sign of this yet-to-be-given land, then, was its ratification by circumcision (v. 11). In both instances the key element was not an animal sacrifice,[17] but rather it was God's spoken voice, the stipulation he made known accompanied by certain symbolic affirmations (i.e., stars, circumcision).

William Barclay leans into covenant writing: "The whole approach comes from God. Man cannot bargain with God; he cannot argue about the terms of the covenant; he can only accept or reject the offer that God makes."[18] Barclay's statement returns us to Genesis, where we find God making a statement on which the entire biblical narrative will pivot. This is heard as God presents the stipulation for living in the garden (2:16–17). As Barclay indicates, that proclamation was not open to negotiation. The man could either accept or reject it (which forms the content of Gen 3). Importantly, God's offer is tied to a symbol, in this case the tree of the knowledge of good and evil, which becomes central to the man's response to God's offer.

It is at this place in the story that verse 18 is significant. The decision to make "a helper suitable for" the man is contextually tied God's proclamation of living in the garden (vv. 16–17). In that sense, the formation of the woman becomes God's sign that ratifies God's covenant with the man as how to live in the garden. Hence, just as God certifies his promise to Abram in Gen 15 with the symbolism of the stars, or in Gen 17 with the act of circumcision, now God certifies this garden covenant with the sign of the

---

16. Kline, *Kingdom Prologue*, 15.

17. Readers must recall that at this point in the narrative there was no need for animal sacrifice; thus the use of such a sacrifice would hold little meaning to Adam.

18. Barclay, *Letter to Hebrews*, 91.

Symmetry in the Second Creation Story

woman. Thus, the woman, who we saw in chapter 6 of this book as comprising the narrative peak of Gen 2, now becomes pivotal in establishing *the theological peak* of Gen 2, which is God's covenant statement.[19]

Two things regarding the garden covenant are important at this point. One is its expression of freedom: the man and the woman are free to eat from any tree in the garden. The second is that the man and the woman are responsible, therefore accountable, for their decisions and actions. They must not eat from the tree of the knowledge of good and evil. Should they do so they will die. Kenneth Matthews forthrightly notes, "But freedom has no meaning without prohibition; the boundary for Adam is but one tree."[20]

Walter Brueggmann,[21] though not writing in a covenant context, nevertheless finds verses 15–17 of Gen 2 holding important significance for human history in three ways. First, the garden is characterized by "vocation"; the man and the woman have work to do. Second, there is "permit"; they are given nearly unlimited freedom. Finally, there is "prohibition"; their freedom has but one restriction. Brueggemann puts it this way: "What counts is the fact of the prohibition, the authority of the one who speaks and the unqualified expectation obedience."[22] Brueggemann concludes, with the future in sight, "The balance and juxtaposition of the three indicate that there is a subtle discernment of human destiny here."[23] Indeed, the story of the paradise garden launches the story of humanity as told through the eyes of ancient Israel. In that telling, humanity's destiny is viewed.

Brueggemann's commentary calls for a decision: will the covenant offer be accepted or rejected? Barclay reminds his readers, referring to Israel's ancient covenant expressed through Moses, that it "offered them a unique relationship" with God. However, that relationship "was entirely dependent on the keeping of the law."[24] Kline understands covenant history as taking the dual forms of "covenant of works" and "covenant of Grace." As a covenant theologian, he takes "the position that the covenant concept can accommodate the entire history of the kingdom of God."[25] It is here

---

19. Kline, *Kingdom Prologue*, 14–21.
20. Matthews, *Genesis 1–11:26*, 211.
21. (ThD, Union Theological Seminary; PhD, St. Louis University; Professor Emeritus OT, Columbia Seminary.)
22. Brueggemann, *Genesis*, 46.
23. Brueggemann, *Genesis*, 46.
24. Barclay, *Letter to Hebrews*, 91.
25. Kline, *Kingdom Prologue*, 14.

that the importance of Jeremy Treat's understanding of covenant enters our discussion. Treat writes, "God administers his kingdom through the covenants."[26] Putting all this together, what occurs in the garden between God and the man is a covenant.

With that background, figure 23 demonstrates that what occurs in the garden segment is the passage's peak. Therefore, viewing this passage symmetrically, it is balanced between God's instructions on how to live in the garden, coming in the middle—or peak—of the passage, up against the formation of the man and the woman, who look to the covenant for instruction. Hence, theologically, this segment holds important context for understanding the creation story, established now through God's covenant, with the coming drama of the garden.

SUMMARY

We began this chapter by discussing Hebrew writing and how it afforded listeners important cues for understanding. Basic to this was employment of literary structure. In the previous chapter, having identified one such structure, linear, in this chapter focus turned to symmetrical structure. In contrast to linear—which places climax at a writing's end—symmetrical structure positions an author's most important statements in the middle.

With that in mind, we examined Gen 2's middle segment and found God's covenant instructions telling the human couple how to live in the paradise garden. Read this way, the passage's symmetry returns readers (and listeners) to God and to what he has to say about living in relationship with him.

In the coming chapters, symbol words will be examined. One is garden trees and the fruit they bear; another is how the author uses the word "marriage." Closure comes by examining the word "serpent," found in Gen 3. To aid this examination, a special insert on ancient communication follows.

Genre and the Creation Stories

The importance of genre to understanding a biblical text is discovered once we turn from straightforward reading to interpretation. This reflective pause is guided by the tension between what Gen 1 and 2 report and how

---

26. Treat, *Crucified King*, 129.

today's scientific thinking looks at origins. The content of Gen 2—aided by word-images, such as magical trees which offer hope of life immortal and a talking serpent—points to the literary question of genre. Bruce Waltke discusses this as he writes, "For most, however, the attempt to harmonize the scientific data with a straight-forward reading of Genesis is not credible, and as a result the Bible's message is rejected as a viable option in the marketplace of competing world-and life-views."[27]

Observations like Waltke's are the backbone of the hermeneutic debate reviewed at the start of this book. Jud Davis points to this as he notes, "Within evangelicalism over the last two centuries, a number of OT [Old Testament] scholars, if not a majority, have resolved this antinomy [i.e., controversy] by suggesting that the Bible does not teach the traditional/plain-language view."[28]

In selecting this quote, I chose Professor Davis because he too, like so many evangelicals, is caught in a riptide that pulls and drags at the church's interpretation of the creation stories. In a remarkably honest baring of his own quandary he wonders, "Is the traditional view (if there is a traditional view) harmful to evangelicalism?"[29] He further writes, "I feel the power of this new majority view: if it proves correct, such a view would remove a stumbling block to the faith. Christians could then say to the scientific intelligentsia, 'We do not believe that the Bible means to support young earth creationism . . .'"[30] Davis then expresses his own view, declining to give way to what it appears that he knows, or seemingly yearns to believe. "I am glad for evangelical thinkers willing to forward such views. I wish that I believed that such was the teaching of Gen 1, but I cannot."[31]

Like Professor Davis, I too felt that tidal pull, the tension between wanting to and, indeed, affirming the literalness of the Genesis text. But unlike Professor Davis, in my search to understand I found more than sufficient reason to support a different interpretation than that traditionally offered by conservative readers. Among those reasons is genre.

Professor John Walton, in a discussion involving hermeneutics, genre, and literal interpretation, points out that "we still need to discover what claims the biblical author is making."[32] He elaborates: "We are not using a

---

27. Waltke, *Dance*, 163.

28. Davis, "Unresolved Major Questions," 209. (PhD, University of Sheffield; Professor of Greek, Bryan College.)

29. Davis, "Unresolved Major Questions," 207.

30. Davis, "Unresolved Major Questions," 209.

31. Davis, "Unresolved Major Questions," 209.

32. Walton, "Four Responses to Chapter Two," 70.

'figurative hermeneutic'—we are trying to understand as best as we are able precisely what the biblical author intends to communicate."[33] For Walton, this intermix comes down to affirming "that all ANE [ancient Near Eastern] literature (not just myth) gives us access to the way that people typically thought in the ancient world and that Israel often would have thought the same way."[34]

Determining genre and meaning, hence, first begins by considering the culture in which writing exists. Further, the text itself supplies readers with important clues. For example, if Genesis had begun, "Once upon a time,[35] God created the universe . . ." we would immediately classify its genre as a fairy tale. Or if it started, "This is the official log of how God created the universe," we would have reason to read it as a statement of history. Or if the biblical writer had elected, "In the cosmos, the forces of energy and matter had so compacted, drawn in by gravitational dynamics . . ." then the discipline of science would come to mind. But none of these illustrations are how the text begins. By immediately naming God as subject of the opening seven-word statement, the author informs its genre: it pertains to the supernatural world of God, which casts Genesis's genre as theology—the study and learning about the Divine Being.

Further, as we continue into the text, we encounter a natural order that is described through words and images that bear no connection to the known world; thus we hear of trees whose fruit gives wisdom and immortality. We read of a serpent figure (compelling us to wonder what a serpent is!) and know without question that we have entered the region's way of expressing ideas through myth. Putting these two claims together—theology and myth—along with the Near East's preference to express creation in terms of functionality and order,[36] then surely, we have come a long way in establishing a classification for Gen 1–11's writing style.

Charles Halton wrote, alluding to Galileo, that he "thought that these passages [the early chapters of Genesis] should be interpreted not according to their strict, grammatical meaning but according to a different set of rules; rules that take into account the complexities of communication such as metaphor, symbolism, and imagery . . ."[37] Halton, quoting Galileo, notes that Scripture's literal text often means "things which are quite

---

33. Walton, "Four Responses to Chapter Two," 70.

34. Walton, "Four Responses to Chapter Two," 71.

35. Compare to Halton and Gundry, *Genesis*, 16.

36. See Walton, *Genesis One*, "Proposition 2," entitled "Ancient Cosmology Is Function Oriented," 21.

37. Halton and Gundry, *Genesis*, 14.

different from what its bare words signify."³⁸ His point: often Scripture's "bare words" requires us to "read the Bible with sensitivity towards its various genres."³⁹

Halton continues, contending that "both author and reader must share the same code, the same system of representing meaning in graphical form."⁴⁰ In other words, understanding a written text requires appreciation of its literary types as well as the culture from which it emerged. However, with Genesis, that is problematic, given conservative Christianity's preference to read it as history-science set within Western culture. Halton inquires, "But what happens when we leave our culture and inhabit a different one, a culture that may or may not have the same rules and expectations that govern its genres, and may even have entirely different genres that those we are familiar with?"⁴¹

In a discussion on genre, Halton considers the necessity of readers to arrive at (some) determination of a story's literary type. He writes, "Readers will first need to understand the genre of the text and how it worked within the author's cultural environment before they will be able to successfully address the question: 'What does this text mean?'"⁴²

It is clear, then, that Genesis's early chapters contain some form of myth. But for many, "myth" is popularly thought of as fable. James Hoffmeier cites, "There is a long tradition of regarding myth to be fiction."⁴³ To recalibrate that idea, Hoffmeier borrows from Mircea Eliade, who considers that "myth narrates a sacred history."⁴⁴ Hoffmeier clarifies, "The key idea here is that myth deals with what 'really happened.'"⁴⁵

Emphasis on how exactly myth portrays what "really happened," though, is up for debate. For example, Tremper Longman finds Genesis employing an "obviously figurative language . . . and the text's pervasive interplay with ANE creation accounts indicate that we are not getting a

---

38. Halton and Gundry, *Genesis*, 14.
39. Halton and Gundry, *Genesis*, 15.
40. Halton and Gundry, *Genesis*, 15.
41. Halton and Gundry, *Genesis*, 17.
42. Halton and Gundry, *Genesis*, 18.
43. Hoffmeier and Millard, "Genesis 1–11 as History and Theology," 26. (Hoffmeier: PhD, University of Toronto; OT scholar, archaeologist, and Egyptologist; Professor OT, Trinity International University.)
44. Hoffmeier and Millard, "Genesis 1–11 as History and Theology," 27.
45. Hoffmeier and Millard, "Genesis 1–11 as History and Theology," 27.

Beyond Myth

literal or precise depiction of these events."[46] He adopts "theological history" as genre for Gen 1–2.[47]

Others use similar but slightly different labels, such as "protohistory"[48] or "mytho-historical," employed by Thorkild Jacobsen and quoted by Gordon Wenham.[49] Then there are those like Kenton Sparks, who find that the early chapters of Genesis "could never yield dependable history or modern science."[50] Regardless of where on the "myth spectrum" a reader elects to place "history," it is evident that (a) Genesis is using mythic images and by doing so (b) those images have in mind some form of history-telling, that is, a "historical impulse"[51] (whether representational or actual) that occurred in a deeper, more distant past. In that sense, Kenton Sparks offers a realistic appraisal of the biblical story: "We will do far better if we honor the humble medium of Scripture and try, as best we can, to listen to what the ancient authors were trying to say through that medium."[52]

Reading the garden story as myth or myth-like permits us to see Scripture through the eyesight of those who wrote it. Further, by attending to how the biblical author organized the creation story by structural nuances, we come closer to decoding the text's bare words than we would do otherwise. The biblical writer wrote to convey theological concepts and ideas, but he did so from within a stylized, ancient communication. When Gen 3 begins, "Now the serpent was more crafty than any of the wild animals the Lord God had made," it is not necessary for believers to defend the idea that in the garden of God there was an actual beast who walked and talked, acting with subtle deception. Kenton Sparks puts it this way: "If Genesis is the word of God, as I and other Christians believe, then we must try to understand how God speaks through a narrative that is no longer the literal history that our Christian forebearers often assumed it to be."[53]

Why these genre arguments are often rejected, though, has much to do with our own faith culture and the insistence that God would not communicate origins as myth. It is not the text, however, that is the stumbling block but us. By limiting God to our preferred method of

---

46. Longman, "What Genesis 1–2 Teaches (and Doesn't)," 109.
47. Longman, "What Genesis 1–2 Teaches (and Doesn't)," 109.
48. Wenham, "Genesis 1–11 as Protohistory," 87.
49. Wenham, "Genesis 1–11 as Protohistory," 87.
50. Sparks, "Genesis 1–11 as Ancient Historiography," 139.
51. Longman, "What Genesis 1–2 Teaches (and Doesn't)," 109
52. Sparks, "Genesis 1–11 as Ancient Historiography," 139.
53. Sparks, "Genesis 1–11 as Ancient Historiography," 111.

communication—history-writing—we have missed the obvious fact that the biblical writer wrote out of his cognitive world and its way of expressing truth-claims.

We find, then, Gen 1–11 to be written in a style that corresponds to what and how Israel and the region of that time thought, wrote, and believed about beginnings. For them to factually say that a serpent walked and talked, or that animals lined up in orderly ranks and padded into a waiting ark, or that "wild animals" (2:19–20) meekly waited next to animals they preyed upon, and then to conclude that we must comprehend such truth-claims as "history" is surely to miss the mark. Once we allow ourselves the freedom to acknowledge that textual statements like these are part of mythical and theological genres, then we are prepared to read Gen 1–11 authentically, as would the audience for whom the biblical author wrote, which was ancient Israel.

Bernhard Anderson finds the task of the biblical "interpreter is to demythologize the world view of the Bible . . . into terms that modern persons can appreciate."[54] He continues, "Moreover, we know that the Bible is not written in the kind of language in which words represent the precise sense of factual proposition (Wittgenstein)."[55] Comparing the message of the biblical writer to a dance, Anderson quotes R. R. Marett:

> But even when thought out, religion is focused in the verbal equivalence of the dance: myth, symbol, and metaphor. To insist on assigning to it a literal, one-dimensional meaning is to shrink and stifle and distort the significance.[56]

Conclusion

The purpose of this reflection is to place before readers evidence that the two creation stories (indeed, most of Gen 1–11) were written in literary genres containing large parts of mythical communication. However, if fundamentalists continue to resist that reality, they place limits on the biblical writer's intent and chosen method to communicate his message. Rather than oppose that conclusion, we should embrace Scripture for what it is and not constrain it, forcing it to say what we desire it to say and by our preferred means. After all, truth is available through myth as well as history writing. Thus, we are left to ponder why it is that we continue to insist that *the Divine Author* behind the inspired text be limited by a twenty-first-century culture's preference for revealing truth.

---

54. Anderson, *Creation Versus Chaos*, 181.
55. Anderson, *Creation Versus Chaos*, 181.
56. Anderson, *Creation Versus Chaos*, 181–82.

CHAPTER 8

Garden Images: "Tree" as Symbol Word

GENESIS 2 AND 3, as ancient texts, describe trees bearing fruit capable of imparting knowledge and address a speaking serpent. Such declarations are consistent with how ancient people in the Near East considered their world. In our present culture, though, we know that fruit does not impart knowledge; neither does a serpent talk. Knowing that, however, does not reduce Genesis's passages to fantasy and make-believe. Rather, in Israel's (mythical) stylized stories, today's readers gain insight into truth-claims made by the biblical author about Yahweh and humanity.

In the previous two chapters, emphasis was on biblical structure. In this and the following chapter, our focus shifts to author style and how repeated words convey meaning. But first, attention is given to translating Bibles into English from Hebrew. The need for this is driven by conflicts that arise between Bible translations over words and thoughts, and in this chapter's examination, the number of times a specific word is repeated in a passage. Here, the word "tree" is spotlighted as an example of such interpretative challenges.

TRANSLATION AND INTERPRETATION OF ANCIENT TEXTS

To understand Gen 2, we need to recognize the importance of cultural context. Of that John Walton writes, "In the ancient world they are more likely to think of the world in terms of *symbols* and to express their understanding by means of *imagery* (emphasis added)."[1] In that world there

1. Walton, *Lost World of Adam and Eve*, 136.

Garden Images: "Tree" as Symbol Word

was a fundamental difference between how people thought and expressed ideas than how we do today. While we rely on factual evidence and science, the ancients employed literary figures and stylized words to express what they knew and believed. Hence, Walton's concluding statement bears attention: "We have to take care not to impose our categories of thinking on the literature that was more at home in the ancient world than is ours."[2] One challenge, though, in reading ancient texts written in other languages is how modern English Bibles translate Israel's ancient scrolls.

Bible Versions, Translations, and Interpretation

One example of difficulties Bible translators face when translating from Hebrew to English pertains to word choice; not all Bibles, as we've seen, select the same words to express ideas. For example, some versions prefer "firmament" over "sky" or elect "vault" when describing the earth's atmosphere. A reason for such discrepancies stems from decisions that Bible boards make about the type of Bible they intend to produce.

Broadly speaking, there are different types of Bibles available to boards when translating Hebrew into English. One choice is to produce a highly readable English version by rephrasing the ancient Hebrew language. In this method, translators distill a Hebrew text's main ideas at the paragraph and story level. That extract is then put into readable English paragraphs. As a result, attention is not directed toward strong correspondences based on word-for-word correlations. An example of this type of Bible is The Message. Another popular Bible in this mode that is now decades-old and largely out-of-print is the Living Bible. Bibles of this type are referred to as paraphrases.

To avoid some of the pitfalls common to paraphrases, translators whose aim is to capture the precision of the original language do so by translating a Hebrew text at a smaller unit of meaning, such as a sentence or a clause. This kind of translation generally provides a nice balance between readability and statement accuracy. For several decades, the New International Version (NIV) has been a standout of this type of Bible. Another example, of more recent vintage, is the New English Translation (NET); it has earned a reputation for scholarly accuracy while maintaining a readable text.

---

2. Walton, *Lost World of Adam and Eve*, 139.

Other versions, however, prefer an even more controlled correspondence between Hebrew and English. This sort utilizes, as much as possible, word-for-word correlations.[3] Here, the New American Standard Bible (NASB) serves as a bellwether model. A challenge these versions face, though, can be a degradation in readability.

In *Beyond Myth*, employment of literary structure and author style as key tools of interpretation works best with Bibles that are translations and not paraphrases. Yet, even within translations, there can be tensions between accuracy and readability when one version is compared to another. Previously, we saw that in the dispute over *tanninim*'s translation. This situation occurs in Gen 2 and the word "tree."

Tree, Translation, and Symbol Meaning

The word "tree" is found six times in some clause- and sentence-oriented Bible translations. For example, the NIV places "tree" four times into Gen 2 as cited below in verse 9, and then in verse 16 it is twice-listed. To illustrate this, the word "tree" is intentionally italicized below.

> **9** The Lord God made all kinds of *trees* grow out of the ground— *trees* that were pleasing to the eye and good for food. In the middle of the garden were the *tree* of life and the *tree* of the knowledge of good and evil.
>
> **16** And the Lord God commanded the man, "You are free to eat from any *tree* in the garden; **17** but you must not eat from the *tree* of the knowledge of good and evil, for when you eat from it you will certainly die."

Yet, when a word-for-word version is consulted, such as the NASB, "tree" is translated five rather than six times.

> **9** Out of the ground the Lord God caused every *tree* to grow that is pleasing to the sight and good for food; the *tree* of life was also in the midst of the garden, and the *tree* of the knowledge of good and evil.
>
> **16** The Lord God commanded the man, saying, "From any *tree* of the garden you may freely eat; **17** but from the *tree* of the

---

3. The two types of translations (not paraphrases) noted here are sentence- or clause-based and word-for-word. These are more commonly described in the scholarly world as "dynamic-equivalence" (e.g., thought-for-thought) and "formal-equivalence" (e.g., "literal"). For elaboration see the Bible Translation Committee, "Introduction," A11.

knowledge of good and evil you shall not eat, for on the day that you eat from it you will certainly die."

The issue we face then is how such a subtle difference might affect understanding this passage. It some instances, such discrepancies might not seem that important. However, when readers seek a level of understanding that conforms to the cryptic phrase "deep calls to deep," such seemingly small differences can lead to important alterations in a passage's interpretation. Having explored several resources to help resolve this issue, which is "should 'tree' be read five times or six?," the view adopted here is that "tree" is most likely found five times in the original language text.[4] What this means for interpretative analysis is discussed below.

"Tree" Five Times

One means in which biblical numbers aid interpretation is through what is termed a "callback." Callbacks occur when repeated words, images, or similar ideas can be traced back to prior usages. To illustrate this concept, we will come to see how the flood in Gen 6 connects readers back to Gen 1, with its description of the primordial sea. In that correspondence, water covered the land's surface. In other words, a callback acts like a conveyor belt, transporting one idea back to a previous or similar usage; hence the flooding waters of Gen 6 equate to the all-covering waters of Gen 1:2.

When the Genesis author made repeated reference to "tree," it is inconceivable that such repeated usage was coincidental. Here the employment of "tree" alerts readers to an intentional callback. In Gen 1 the word "separate" is also used five times. This opens the possibility that a callback is being used to connect Genesis chapter 2's fivefold use of "tree" with Gen 1's fivefold "separate." Hence, this callback is based on biblical numbers. Such symmetry is reason to wonder how textual understanding might be affected.

To begin our investigation into this numbered callback, we start with Bill Arnold. He writes of God's fivefold separating work in Gen 1 by pointing to the Hebrew verbs "do" and "make." He finds that those words acquire

---

4. I am indebted to my excellent copyeditor for alerting me to the question as to whether "tree" is used five or six times. Reviewing the Blue Letter Bible's interlinear Hebrew and English text which prompted this question, examining the Orthodox Jewish Bible, as well as English word-for-word translations, such as the NASB, it is apparent that the most likely original use of "tree" was five times.

a meaning which alludes to "cutting." Arnold explains that "cutting away" expresses the intent of how God is "shaping, or fashioning" each creation day. He writes, "God brings order and shape to his creation, therefore, by dividing and separating, as in light from darkness and waters from waters."[5] Thus, in the context of Gen 1, all of God's first three days push at the removal, that is, the "cutting away" of the primordial darkness. Hence, God's separating activity, highlighted through the number *five*, finds a theological correspondence in Gen 2, in which "tree" is similarly described. Therefore, the fivefold use of "tree" and "separate" point to the Genesis writer's intent.

With this in mind, we are ready to make an informed, though nuanced, interpretation. It appears the Genesis author has employed number meaning in concert with word repetition to foreshadow a critical decision that the man and the woman will soon be asked to make. As beings created in the image of God, they have been ordained as God's proxies to "rule over" all that God has so artfully brought into existence. Specifically, through the nuance of a callback, there is a veiled hint that Adam and Eve must prepare themselves for a confrontation with "darkness." Hence, the figurative use of "tree" sets the stage for the entrance of the serpent into the garden. As God's appointed rulers, Adam and Eve are to keep the garden secure, *separate* from chaos-inducing figures such as the serpent. In other words, they are to cut away any possible influence that an intruder might introduce into the good order of God's sacred temple ground. It is apparent that God's "light" holds no business with evil's "darkness."

Ethical Rulership

At this point, we must understand how the garden's fruit trees message human rulership. When the text directs the man and the woman to avoid a specified fruit, we need to consider how food, in this case fruit, is being used as an instrument of choice to instruct moral and ethical life decisions. How the man and the woman handle Yahweh's covenant command to avoid eating a certain fruit will have a direct bearing on their future life in the garden; it will also profoundly affect the race's destiny.

On the idea that food is a biblical metaphor, one that expresses ethical living, Jacob Milgrom has much to say. Writing in a chapter entitled "The Dietary Laws,"[6] he moves discussion about Israel's prohibitions on

---

5. Arnold, *Genesis*, 37.
6. Milgrom, *Leviticus*, chapter 11, 102–21. (PhD; three honorary degrees; Professor

Garden Images: "Tree" as Symbol Word

food-handling (found in the book of Leviticus) away from Christianity's normal interpretation that such regulations were God's means of installing hygienic practices.[7] In opposition, Milgrom finds that Israel had no understanding of basic hygienic knowledge. Like our discussion on evolution and creation, the science of ancient societies held little knowledge of health safeguards, sanitation, and disease.

Therefore, the existence of hygienic concepts was not the point of the dietary laws. Milgrom writes, "The dietary laws serve as an ethical guide—a system whereby people will not be brutalized by killing animals for their flesh."[8] This teaching is vested in the concept that the life of an animal is found within its "blood" (Lev 17:10-14). Milgrom states, "Because life is inviolable it may not be tampered with indiscriminately."[9] Important to our study, Milgrom directs this teaching back to Gen 1:26, in which is found the word "rule." A logical connection is built, then, between the race's hunger for food and its "hunger for power,"[10] demonstrated as God permits humanity to take and eat animal flesh, thus engaging in animal slaughter. In this concession, God places an ethical prohibition on the race: no meat may be eaten with its lifeblood in it (Lev 9:4). Milgrom concludes, "The Bible's method of taming the killer instinct in humans is none other than its system of dietary laws."[11]

While Milgrom takes several pages to coherently develop a theology between food and ethical life choices, he adds, "Thus from a brief tracing of the history of the blood prohibition and the established slaughtering method, we have seen that the dietary system rests on foundations that are essentially ethical, and ethical in the highest sense. They teach the inviolability of all life . . ."[12] Milgrom concludes this section writing, "The dietary system, then, is the Torah's prerequisite for the ethical life."[13] Milgrom therefore reinterprets Israel's dietary regulations by framing them as an ethical system. In a narrative and theological sense, this is the beginning of how food is used in the Bible as an ethical metaphor.

Emeritus in Biblical Studies, University of California–Berkeley.)

7. See Milgrom, *Leviticus*, 103.
8. Milgrom, *Leviticus*, 104.
9. Milgrom, *Leviticus*, 105.
10. Milgrom, *Leviticus*, 105.
11. Milgrom, *Leviticus*, 103.
12. Milgrom, *Leviticus*, 106.
13. Milgrom, *Leviticus*, 108.

Beyond Myth

Given that food symbolizes ethics, we can apply Milgrom's teaching to understand Gen 2's ban on fruit. In the garden story, ethical behavior is reduced to a single prohibition placed on one tree, against which the man and the woman must respond. Will they continue in the way of God's covenant, or will they depart from it? Their decision, as Milgrom indicated, is an ethical choice "in the highest sense." What they decide will form the basis for the remainder of the Genesis narrative, one that will spread outward and forward, affecting humanity's destiny.

Moving forward in Israel's history, we come upon a slice of that destiny; it resides in a divided nation. Kings pit themselves against priests, and priests seek power over kings, and prophets rant against both. In the end, a kingdom once united under David quickly falls away after Solomon's death, resulting not only in a fractured realm but its eventual destruction.

Fast-forwarding to today, we ask if a match exists between the garden of Eden's fruit and an unbounded quest for political power sought by many in the church.[14] The reason this question is raised is that it echoes a conclusion held by secular American. There is no doubt in the minds of many non-churched citizens (as well as many Christians) that a great divide is taking place in the Christian world, one that has split people of faith into two camps. One segment, desiring power and control as means to "rule over," has sought alliances with political allies[15] whose intent is to bring about a religious-political end that reduces freedom, suppresses people, and in the process limits the receptivity of those on the outside who otherwise might have turned to Christ's "good news." Therefore, the question that needs to be asked—indeed, must be asked—is, How might America's Christians perform the sacred work of "ruling over"?

Russell Moore, editor-in-chief of *Christianity Today* at the time of this writing, exposes this politically induced split in the American church as a large swath of Christians seek to impose political power upon the nation.[16] In other words, is the body of Christ repeating the failed story of Israel that was touched on in the preface? And if we are—as this book postulates—then how might rulership (as laid out in Genesis) instruct our application of the image in which we have been created?

---

14. Kristin Kobes Du Mez outlines the cultural forces that support this contention throughout her book. See Du Mez, *Jesus*.

15. See Du Mez, *Jesus*, in preface, xiii-xix.

16. Moore, "Mount Zion or Mar-a-Lago."

CONCLUSION

To sum up our analysis so far, by focusing on the repeated word "tree," we found correspondence with the word "separate" in Gen 1. Further, by enlisting Bill Arnold, we discovered that "separate" alludes to "cutting away." Thus, much like a conveyor belt, the fivefold use of "separate" in Gen 1, when linked to Gen 2's fivefold employ of "tree," conveys to interpreters this nuanced meaning of separate. The significance of that, then, was found in the role of Adam and Eve as God's appointed rulers. Essentially, they were to cut away the looming figure of darkness and thereby maintain the garden as a sacred site.

Given this, we came to see how the biblical writer was setting the stage for a momentous decision the human couple soon would make. Would they consume the banned fruit, or would they make an ethical decision based on God's covenant, one that leads to the tree of life? Another way to say this is that depending on which fruit is consumed—the banned fruit or the fruit of life—human fitness to act as God's co-rulers hangs in the balance.

CHAPTER 9

Garden Images: "Marriage" and "Serpent" as Symbol Words

THIS CHAPTER CONTINUES TO explore symbol words in Gen 2 and Gen 3. Here we take up "marriage" and "serpent," adding cultural depth to our reading of the second creation story. We begin with "marriage." Though neither this word, nor a "wedding" ceremony is found in the text, nevertheless Adam and Eve's "marriage" is readily affirmed by nearly all New Testament users. The section on marriage is followed by the symbol imagery of "serpent." This chapter closes by connecting the findings from chapter 8 with those of this chapter.

"MARRIAGE" AS SYMBOL WORD

To understand how Gen 2 is using marriage, we need to locate it within its biblical and historic context.[1] While the word "marriage" is not explicitly found in Gen 2, it is implied through the text's sudden reference to the woman as "wife" (see verse 24). This is one reason Bill Arnold may write, "so now Gen 2 concludes with the social institution of marriage."[2] Here, Victor Hamilton considers verse 24's "why a man leaves his father and

---

1. To illustrate the importance that ancient Israel placed on marriage "purity" as part of the nation being a faith community, see for example Ezra 9 and 10 and the back half of chapter 13 in Nehemiah. Importantly, these stories pertain to a post-exilic time, a period in Israel's history in which many biblical scholars believe substantial redactions to the nation's scrolls occurred. See for example Brueggemann, *Genesis*, 24–25, under point 2.

2. Arnold, *Genesis*, 61.

Garden Images: "Marriage" and "Serpent" as Symbol Words

mother and is united to his wife" to be a marriage covenant.[3] Indeed, both writers direct their comments toward a larger goal, namely, the *solidarity of the union of the two becoming one*. This idea is expressly born out in the text itself, as the Genesis author states that the man "is united to his wife."

What is likely happening in these verses, which are part of the story of the woman's formation (vv. 18–24), is that they move the narrative from an isolated man—who is alone and without a like mate—to one who is now gifted with the woman's presence. Thereby the man is suddenly fulfilled; he is co-part of a vibrant relationship with another being of his own kind. Read this way, the text is not so much introducing the sacrament of marriage as it is describing a state of being, the need for humans to be in union with one another. Towner, writing on this same text, puts it this way: "The long-awaited division of *adam* into man and woman is about to take place. God takes the decision to move this way neither in the interest of sexuality nor in the interest of progeny, but in the interest of community."[4]

Conclusions such as these are cause to examine more closely the biblical author's reference to marriage through the word "wife." Structurally, emphasis on wife/marriage comes at the close of Gen 2, where it importantly transitions the story to Gen 3. This occurs through the swift encounter with the serpent as Gen 3 opens. Therefore, Gen 2's emphasis on solidarity, in which two humans are expected to act as though one (community), prepares readers to comprehend the importance of a now-joined together human couple living in solidarity under the Divine Creator's covenant (vv. 15–17). Here, then, is this essential message; it is driven metaphorically by marriage as an image word (vv. 24–25) and it comes just as the serpent is introduced (3:1). It will prove consequential for the couple's capacity to "rule over."

Thus marriage as a metaphor links Gen 1, which also employed poetry to make known the creation of humanity in God's image. In Gen 2 we find the man and the woman described as solidly unified, which is the picture presented by Gen 1:27's use of "them." Genesis 2 poetically states:

> This is now bone of my bones
> and flesh of my flesh;
> she shall be called 'woman,' for she was taken out of man. (v. 23)

---

3. Hamilton, *Book of Genesis*, 181.
4. Towner, *Genesis*, 37.

In essence, the addition of the "marriage" language that immediately follows has the primary effect of reinforcing how the now "married" couple is to act. That is, the two people are to be united as one kin[5] in their administration as rulers over God's sacred garden. The words "man" and "woman" in Hebrew are *ish* ("man") and *ishah* ("woman"); thus their sounds echo and reinforce solidarity. Created and now formed into a oneness, they are prepared to take on the challenges of the garden world. How that turns out is discovered in Gen 3.

Before moving on to the serpent, however, there is need to draw on verse 25, the final verse in Gen 2. It reads, "Adam and his wife were both naked, and they felt no shame." The word "naked," coupled with "felt no shame," is a metaphor that eclipses the implied sexual innocence of the apparently "married" couple. Hence, in the man and the woman's nakedness, God considers them as being without blemish or fault. That statement is no mere comment on the couple's virginal status but rather alludes to their innocence before God. In other words, that condition—the text's "naked" and "not ashamed"—figuratively asserts the text's aim: spotless and without blame before God, which are prerequisite ethical, moral, and spiritual conditions for communion with God.

It is this idyllic state of being that stands behind the nation of Israel's communal rituals, rites, and sacrifices. Of that idea, the book of Leviticus lays out priestly and community regulations. Jacob Milgrom writes, "One can see from the preceding discussion that the ritual complexes of Leviticus 1–16 make sense only as aspects of a symbolic system."[6] As part of that symbolic system are legislations for animal sacrifice. Leviticus requires, "If the offering is a burnt offering from the herd, he [layperson bringing the animal] is to offer a male without defect" (1:3) and then again, "If the offering is a burnt offering from the flock, from either the sheep or the goats, he is to offer a male without defect" (1:10). Whereas the NIV uses "without defect," as does the NASB, the NET elects "flawless." On the other hand, the NRSVUE selects "without blemish." The idea behind these various words is that animals used for sacrifices must be perfect, spotless, leaving the one bringing the offering without cause of embarrassment or feelings of exploitation.[7] Hence, as a sacrifice was burned it gave off a pleasing aroma that

---

5. See NET, study note "bw," Gen 2:23.
6. Milgrom, *Leviticus*, 11.
7. See NET, study note "by," Gen 2:25.

was carried by means of smoke to God's "heavenly throne."[8] The symbolic concept being expressed, therefore, was one of access. Milgrom writes, "For them [the laypersons of ancient Israel], God was personally accessible . . . by means of their sacrifice on the outer altar."[9]

Applied to the garden, it was there that the man and the woman had access to God. We know this because God spoke to the man while walking in the garden. Thus, it was in the "cool of the day" (3:8) that the couple would come face-to-face with God. As two "naked" people, they were not ashamed; they were not encumbered with guilt but were presentable, like in a future time when Israel, as a faith community, would bring unblemished animals to offer. Therefore, regarding Gen 2 and 3, we will do better if we understand that marriage is being used metaphorically to express unity, a oneness pictured through the climactic moment of humanity's most fervent and unifying act.

"SERPENT" AS SYMBOL WORD

When the serpent is taken up it is necessary to travel deep into Israel's initial faith to grasp how it evolved from what Bernhard Anderson calls "creation faith" up against "Exodus-faith."[10] In other words, Israel's creation-faith was far less actual history than that experienced later, specifically the encounter with God at Sinai. Creation-faith often adapted the ancient world's metaphors and symbols, locating them within the nation's language and rituals, such as harvest ceremonies. Frank Moore Cross wrote, "The radical novelty of Israel's early faith was its attempt to shift this center (the centrality of the drama of creation in Near Eastern cults) from creation to historical redemption in the cultic life of the nation."[11] As Israel broke away from Egyptian religious influence and others, such as the Canaanites' devotion to Baal, Israel separated itself from mythical practices and beliefs to those based on historical artifact, such as Yahweh's acts of redemption.

In the early stages of Israel's faith, ideas prevalent throughout the Near East were initially incorporated into the nation's infantile understanding of

8. Milgrom, *Leviticus*, 18.
9. Milgrom, *Leviticus*, 18.
10. Anderson, *Creation Versus Chaos*, 52.
11. Anderson, *Creation Versus Chaos*, 53, quoting Frank Cross (world-renowned scholar; PhD, Harvard University, Professor Emeritus of Hebrew and Other Oriental Languages.)

the God of Creation. Specifically, this can be seen in Gen 1's descriptive language, such as the primordial sea with its covering of darkness. Averbeck alludes to this and other ancient regional practices and beliefs,[12] like chaos, sea monsters, dragons, and serpents. Bernhard Anderson writes of Israel's "many allusions to the struggle with the dragon of chaos (Rahab, Leviathan, the Serpent, Sea, Flood)"[13] and so forth.

Such ideas—common in the wider regional culture—point to a cosmic conflict[14] to be played out in the battle between order and disorder. Indeed, Gen 1 and 2 may be read as Israel's understanding of the God of Creation who was at work to bring order out of disorder.[15] One agent provocateur in this battle was the "serpent." In the region's literature, many references to serpents can be found. John Walton writes, "Serpent symbolism was rich in the ancient Near East."[16] Walton goes on to distill the serpent as a "figure of chaos."[17] Here, Walton aims at understanding this creature as producing confusion, one capable of bringing "deception, misdirection, and troublemaking."[18] Walton argues, "all [of these conditions] are within the purview of chaos creatures."[19]

Bill Arnold is quick to point out that the serpent of Gen 3 is not Satan, as does Westermann,[20] contrary to contemporary Christian thinking about Genesis today. Arnold writes, "However, there is nothing in Israel's Scriptures that would equate the serpent with Satan, especially since ancient Israelites did not embody all evil in a single personage."[21] Continuing, he adds, "The power of snake-imagery in the ancient world cannot be denied. Serpents were noted for their wisdom, protection, healing, and knowledge of death."[22] Thus, they came to be worshiped. Arnold cites as example the Canaanite fertility cult. Over time, however, the attributes associated with

---

12. See Averbeck, *Biblical Archaeology*, 337–51.
13. Anderson, *Creation Versus Chaos*, 53.
14. See Averbeck, "Ancient Near Eastern Mythography," 351–54.
15. See Walton, *Lost World of Adam and Eve*, Proposition 14 (128–39).
16. Walton, *Lost World of Adam and Eve*, 129.
17. Walton, *Lost World of Adam and Eve*, 132.
18. Walton, *Lost World of Adam and Eve*, 134.
19. Walton, *Lost World of Adam and Eve*, 134.
20. Westermann, *Genesis*, 22.
21. Arnold, *Genesis*, 62.
22. Arnold, *Genesis*, 62.

Garden Images: "Marriage" and "Serpent" as Symbol Words

serpents gave way to New Testament views which squarely identified Genesis's serpent as a figure of evil, even one cast as Satan.[23]

Yet, there is a wider, even more destructive view that may be granted to the serpent than merely introducing chaos and confusion. Walton hints as much, writing with reference to Richard Averbeck, though he pulls back from Averbeck's willingness to equate Genesis's serpent with the fall of Satan.[24]

Turning then to Averbeck, we conclude this short foray into the symbolism of the ancient serpent. In a section entitled "Genesis 3 and the Cosmic Battle,"[25] Averbeck states, "The fact of the matter is that there is more to the serpent in Genesis 3 than has generally been recognized."[26] What Averbeck holds in mind are the "parallels between poetic texts in the Hebrew Bible and the mythological ideas and motifs expressed in the Ugaritic Baal myth."[27] These reveal "the theme of a cosmic battle between God and a serpentine monster bent on evil."[28]

The direction Averbeck takes on a future cosmic battle, then, is aimed at rulership, that is, the sovereign control of creation by God up and against the challenge of evil's chaos figures, such as the serpent. He continues, "Moreover, this serpent issued a direct challenge to the Lord's truthfulness and authority (3:1–5), and the Lord responded with a curse that involved crushing the serpent's 'head.'"[29]

Averbeck's ideas provide background to comprehend Gen 1 (the first story of creation) and Gen 2–3 (the second story of creation). Importantly he describes this as expressing "two different ways of articulating"[30] the Genesis creation narratives. Of that interpretive nuance he writes, "The challenge, and so also the battle between God and the serpent, is actually over mankind. *People are the battleground—the 'territory' under dispute—* and the central concern of this battle of the ages has as much to do with people as with the great serpent."[31] In this, Averbeck points to the effects

---

23. Towner, *Genesis*, 43. See also Arnold, *Genesis*, 42, "as Satan."
24. Walton, *Lost World of Adam and Eve*, 133.
25. See Averbeck, "Ancient Near Eastern Mythography," 351–54.
26. Averbeck, "Ancient Near Eastern Mythography," 351.
27. Averbeck, "Ancient Near Eastern Mythography," 351.
28. Averbeck, "Ancient Near Eastern Mythography," 351.
29. Averbeck, "Ancient Near Eastern Mythography," 352.
30. Averbeck, "Ancient Near Eastern Mythography," 354.
31. Averbeck, "Ancient Near Eastern Mythography," 354.

stemming from the serpent's invasion of the paradise garden and its effect on God's appointed human rulers. That outcome, which is seen in Gen 3, will become central for God's entrance into the history of humanity and the ensuing story of salvation.[32]

The Fall

The above background returns us to the serpent and its role in the garden. Modern Christian tradition is quick to interpret the "fall" of Adam and Eve as a direct influence of the serpent, who is widely and arguably the voice of Satan.[33] From this dogma comes an association of "fall" with the word "sin" and "rebellion," though neither, nor other words such as "transgression," appear in Gen 3.

When viewing the "fall" as sin, two approaches may be considered. One is long-range, which is expressed canonically within the full extent of Christian interpreters, such as Paul, who readily embrace the events in the garden as "sin," going so far as to create an analogy of Adam/Christ.[34] This is standard Christian orthodoxy. However, when viewed within the context of the Genesis story, counter arguments may suggest otherwise, questioning the establishment of "sin" and "fall" here. Thus, Brueggmann may write, this text is "not decisive" and that it is "an exceedingly marginal text."[35] Walton understands the importance of Genesis 3's omission of not casting this event under these labels.[36] He, like Brueggemann, work the "fall" as a reflection on human knowledge and God's wisdom.[37]

Perhaps, then, what is occurring in the garden, of which the serpent is a chaos agent, is a question not so much of sin but wisdom ethics:[38] the eth-

---

32. Viewed from the lens of atonement theology, this position lines up with *Christus Victor*. See Treat, *Crucified King*, 174–77. For an expansive look at Christus Victor, see Boyd, "Christus Victor View," 23–49.

33. Arnold, *Genesis*, 62.

34. See for example, Rom 5:12–14 and 1 Cor 15:21–22; 45–47.

35. Brueggemann, *Genesis*, 41.

36. Walton, *Lost World of Adam and Eve*, 142.

37. See Brueggemann, *Genesis*, 51; further, Walton, *Lost World of Adam and Eve*, 143–44. Also see Arnold, *Genesis*, 63. For Brueggemann and Walton's complete discussions, see Brueggemann, *Genesis*, 40–54; Walton, *Lost World of Adam and Eve*, 140–48.

38. Arnold, Moberly, and Walton all refer to wisdom within the context of the "fall" story. See Arnold, *Genesis*, 63; Moberly, *Theology of Genesis*, 87; Walton, *Lost World of Adam and Eve*, 143–44.

Garden Images: "Marriage" and "Serpent" as Symbol Words

ics implied by a race created in the "image of God" but now being tempted to dissolve the unifying bond of covenant relationship.

At the heart of this issue is trust. Kenneth Matthews writes, "The tactic used by the serpent was to cause doubt . . ."[39] Averbeck leans into this but adds a twist as he writes, "Genesis 3 is indeed a 'fall' narrative, a 'falling out' with God on the part of the serpent and humankind."[40] It is that "falling out" which will dominate the remainder of the biblical text, both Old and New Testaments, until final resolution comes as the book of Revelation ends. Furthermore, David Atkinson sees a connection between "trust" and "doubt," recalling Erik Erikson's eight stages of human development.[41] Holding in mind stage one (trust versus mistrust), Atkinson declares, "The Tempter moves from casting doubt on God's trustworthiness ('Did God say . . . ?') to casting doubt on the truth of his word ('You will not die')."[42]

For our purposes, the "fall" is best understood within two contexts. One is the story's genre, which is set upon the myths of the ancient Near East, which, as Averbeck claims, is "myth as analogical thinking about history and realty."[43] In other words, this puts humanity "right in the (historical) middle of a ferocious cosmic battle," one that "depends on Yahweh's willingness to redeem us in the midst of this brawl."[44]

The second context is the role of humanity as God's image-bearers, royal overseers of the planet and all its life forms, indeed, of its very good and sacred environment. How the race rules, be that in the highest levels of governance, in corporate board rooms, through important, even controversial court decisions (e.g., the president has nearly unrestricted immunity, deportation, abortion, etc.), right down to schoolrooms, hospitals, centers that support homelessness, and even into the living rooms of families, all forms of rulership are caught up in this cosmic battle of deception, chaos, and truth. The ethics the church brings to this battle, currently one fraught with political entanglements,[45] has much to say about the church's effectiveness or ineffectiveness to spread Christ's good news.

---

39. Matthews, *Genesis 1–11:26*, 235.

40. Averbeck, "Ancient Near Eastern Mythography," 355.

41. The eight stages are basic trust, autonomy, initiative, industry, identity, intimacy, generativity, and ego integrity.

42. Atkinson, *Message of Genesis 1–11*, 85.

43. Averbeck, "Ancient Near Eastern Mythography," 35

44. Averbeck, "Ancient Near Eastern Mythography," 354.

45. Du Mez widens entanglements beyond political scandals in chapter 16,

For that reason, the Genesis creation stories may be read as presenting a "test" question: will the human life form that has been granted the god-like gift of freedom of will elect to use that power for good in ruling over the created order, thereby certifying itself as referential image-bearers, suitable as God's proxies . . . or not? Turning to R. W. L. Moberly, this question is framed as *trust*.

> The fact that the serpent never tells the woman to transgress but rather undermines God's trustworthiness and truthfulness, leaving her to draw her own conclusions, points to the real core of human alienation from God and the real root of disobedience—not that God and humans can no longer converse, but rather the difficulty that the human heart and mind can have in genuinely trusting God as a wise creator and living accordingly.[46]

This conclusion tracks well with Milgrom's ethical consideration of the dietary laws and the garden prohibition. Here, in the garden, the human couple face their first ethical decision. It is directly tied to God's appointment as rulers. In that commissioning they were delegated to keep safe God's sacred creation. How they handle that responsibility is of paramount importance; the outcome of the garden question will establish a theological paradigm for the race. Framed by food, the serpent challenges human solidarity with God. Raised is a question the human pair have never contemplated: will they abandon Yahweh's standard for living in the sacred temple land? Will they exchange God's covenant, which expresses God's *lifeview*, rejecting and replacing it with the *worldview*[47] of the serpent, which is a view founded on not trusting God.

Kenton Sparks puts it this way: "In our own day, and presumably throughout the drama of history, human beings have experienced the world as a confusing blend of blessing and curse, good and evil, beauty and obscenity. And as a rule, we have a deep sense that this is not how things should be."[48] Sparks continues, "The serpent deceived the first couple with lies, and they believed his word rather than God's."[49] The unwillingness to

---

"Evangelical Mulligans: A History." See Du Mez, *Jesus and John Wayne*, 272–94.

46. Moberly, *Theology of Genesis*, 86.

47. The two words *lifeview* and *worldview* represent separate paradigms for living. They will be become templates to understand the conflict between God and an adversary in the next and following chapters of this series.

48. Sparks, "Genesis 1–11 as Ancient Historiography," 124.

49. Sparks, "Genesis 1–11 as Ancient Historiography," 124.

Garden Images: "Marriage" and "Serpent" as Symbol Words

trust God, therefore, is an existential threat which requires a decision from all, not just the garden's "man" and "woman."

It was that very lack of trusting, a failure to not believe God and his goodness, that led humanity to reject the marriage metaphor's emphasis on solidarity with God and union with one another. Having made their decision, the man and the woman turned away from Yahweh and were faced with confusion, chaos, and the utter despair of alienation, all attributes of living life within the captive bonds of deception.

CONCLUSION

In this chapter and the preceding one, three symbolic images were examined from the standpoint of the ancient world. The first was the relationship between the garden's two trees and the question of which fruit would be eaten. As understood through Milgrom's work on Leviticus, that decision—framed as an ethical response to God's covenant—is rooted in humanity's willingness to either trust or not trust the Creator.

The second symbol word was "marriage." It expressed the vital importance of the man and the woman, by virtue of marriage, to be of one mind and one community, grounded in God and his goodness. But even more so, reference to the man and the woman's unashamed nakedness depicts their state of being as blameless innocence. In that condition they have full access to God.

Finally, serpent imagery gives rise to a cosmic conflict over God's creation. In Gen 1, God's creation activity reversed "darkness" and its life-suppressing conditions that were imposed on earth's landscape, which lay beneath an all-covering sea. This figuration is best understood within the biblical context of a cosmic battle. In that campaign, war is waged between God and all foes aligned against him. That "battle," however, is not contested on earth's "dry" ground but rather on the cosmic terrain of humanity itself, beings created in the image and likeness of God. At issue is whether a now naked and ashamed race can once more return to trusting God.

By understanding the meaning of image-words and symbols, a pathway to authentically read Genesis opens. By this means, the creation story shifts from beyond myth to truth-telling; from alienation and loneliness to unity and harmony; and from mythic gods and beings from another dimension to the reality of spiritual warfare, fought not so much in the heavenlies but anchored here, on terrestrial earth. Such a background prepares modern readers to enter God's garden in Eden, a sacred site informed through the image of a cosmic temple in which the Creator has placed the man and the woman, whom he dearly loves.

In the coming chapter we will encounter the serpent and observe the chaos he renders, making note of the devastation he brings to all, not just to this single man and the woman. Framed in this manner, we will observe chaos's effect on humanity's charge to "rule over."

CHAPTER 10

Into the Garden

PASSAGE RETELL

Like a television series, Gen 3 opens with a stunning teaser. Immediately we hear the moderator exclaim, "Now the serpent was more crafty than any of the wild animals the Lord God had made." Viewers urgently await first sightings of this mysterious creature—who is it; what does it look like? Although the crafty animal is masked from physical description, the episode's plot, in contrast, quickly comes into focus as the beast speaks. He addresses the newest star, "Did God really say, 'You must not eat from any tree in the garden'?" Strangely, the text does not explain why the moderator has dropped the star's title, "wife" (see 2:25). In its place, reference is made to gender (woman—"*ishshah*"—in Hebrew).

After the teaser concludes, this new episode moves swiftly. We learn that the "good" union in which the husband and the wife were depicted at the close of chapter 2 is now in doubt. The story's author splits the couple's oneness as he places the man into a secondary role, that of listener. Hence, the man remains off-center stage as the cunning animal proffers an array of confusing questions, all directed at the woman. In that encounter the wild animal reveals its game plan: deception. Its aim is to transform the woman's lifeview, held in God's goodness, to the serpent's worldview, forged in darkness. Step by step, the beast succeeds. Complicit in this exchange is the man; he stands silently by, just off-stage, watching.

Completely drawn in and over her head, the woman inches closer to what the serpent wants. Her sight becomes radicalized as she increasingly desires the tree's fruit. This occurs as she comes to believe that the banned fruit is "good for food" but more so is "desirable for gaining wisdom." Suddenly she lunges, plucking some from the tree of the "knowledge of good and evil." As she eats, she hands some to her husband; both savor the desired but banned food.

No sooner is the enticing fruit devoured than a strange feeling overcomes the couple. It is almost as if they have never truly seen one another, and rather embarrassed, the man and the woman hastily cover themselves with fig leaves. Moreover, the sound of Yahweh walking in the garden is cause for panic—they have disobeyed his injunction. Quickly they flee into the thick foliage, desperate to find a hiding place.

Events move rapidly. They are discovered, and in that moment, like a swirling nightmare filled with confusing imagery, the garden becomes a courtroom. Yahweh, their friend, is now their judge. The man and the woman are disoriented; they resort to blaming in a failed attempt to excuse their conduct. For a moment this tactic seems to work. Yahweh has located and brought to the courtroom the strange creature who is called "the serpent." A sentence is rendered. Eerily the woman's skin crawls in anticipation of its fulfillment. In some distant future an offspring of the serpent will collide violently with one of her children. It is too ghastly to contemplate. The man and the woman now come under Yahweh's indictment. They will die. But first a life sentence must be served; it will be a penalty filled with toil and pain.

The trial over, the man, who is now called Adam, grants his wife a name. She is to be known as Eve, which means "living" (or mother of life). Further, Yahweh, in an extraordinary act they do not fully comprehend, makes clothing, removing their fig leaves and fitting them with animal skins. The trial terminates, and Adam and Eve are banned from the garden. Exiting, they risk a look back hoping to find a way of return. But the entrance is blocked by a fearsome being, one they have never seen before. He stands guard, powerfully brandishing a "flaming sword," swishing and twirling, flashing it back and forth. For Adam and Eve there is only one pathway and so turning their backs upon the cherubim-guard, they walk eastward . . . toward an unknown horizon.

IN THIS CHAPTER, THE garden drama is taken up. Examination of its overall structure reveals three segments. A closer inspection, though, finds the passage formed out of sub-structures, or what may be termed "microstructures." Seen from this micro level, the story's stylistic details gain interpretative prominence; noteworthy is the identity of Yahweh, who takes on the role of a cosmic investigator and judge. In the end, we learn that Gen 3 is not about sin and rebellion and "fall" so much as it is about transforming the couple's view of life, jerking them away from the wisdom of trusting God and vesting them with evil's knowledge.

STRUCTURE AND STYLE IN THE SECOND CREATION STORY

Three scenes, depicted in figure 26, outline Genesis 3's overall structure. The drama begins as the serpent deceives the woman in the garden. This act of disobedience shifts the story from its garden setting to a courtroom-like scene in which the three actors (serpent, woman, and man) are indicted and sentenced. The story's conclusion comes at the eastern edge of the garden.

FIGURE 26. THREE SCENES IN THE PARADISE DRAMA

Scene 1	Scene 2	Scene 3
Garden Deception (vv. 1–13)	Courtroom Judgments (vv. 14–19)	Garden Expulsion (vv. 20–24)

Further, the chapter's triadic structure is refined by *microstructures*. Microstructures break a text's larger, overall structure into smaller presentations. In Gen 3, the first scene in the garden occurs in two phases. The second scene, which takes place in a "cosmic courtroom," is refined by three trial events. The final scene, though, in which the two humans are evicted from the garden, occurs without one.

FIGURE 27. STRUCTURE AND MICROSTRUCTURE IN GEN 3

Garden Deception	Courtroom	Garden Expulsion

Microstructures in Genesis 3

Serpent deceives the Woman	Yahweh confronts the man and the woman	Serpent on Trial (vss. 14-15)	Woman on Trial (v. 16)	Man on Trial (vss. 17-19)

Beyond Myth

First Scene: Garden Deception

Microstructure: Serpent Deceives the Woman

Beginning with the first scene, *the garden deception*, it is formed out of *two* microstructures. This reveals a theological contrast between the serpent and Yahweh, pointing to a startling gap between how the serpent and Yahweh look upon life and ethical living. That difference occurs in the serpent's depiction: he is "crafty." The NET elects "shrewder" over "crafty," which "basically means 'clever'" sprinkled with nuances of "cunning" and "prudence."[1] Thus the text paints this wild animal as deceptive. The serpent, true to its character, engages the woman in a classic bait-and-switch move, which leaves her confused. The conversation begins, "Did God really say . . ." before forcefully contradicting God: "You will not certainly die." The serpent's wily motivation is understood through his remark "your eyes will be opened, and you will be like God, knowing good and evil."

The word for "crafty" (NIV) or "shrewd" (NET) in Hebrew is "*arum*." In this context it forms a Hebrew wordplay. It involves the concepts of "naked" (Hebrew *arummim* in 2:25)—which was the couple's virginal condition—the serpent's shrewdness (3:1), and the couple's transformed "nakedness" (3:7). Taken together, this results in Adam and Eve becoming "shrewd" like the serpent.[2] In other words, the wisdom offered by the serpent lies in contrast to God's wisdom, which is his lifeview.[3] Through the serpent's deceptive phrasing, the creature's motive is identified, which is to expose the couple and impose chaos. The beast desires to break apart the couple's union, especially with God.

Here, the word "naked" (see v. 7) first read in 2:25, is more than a reference to sexual innocence. In the context of the second creation story, the couple's unashamed nakedness is their full acceptance and belief that what God told them is true-Truth. Although they lack experience to know anything more than "goodness," at this point they have no desire or reason to move beyond God's truth-telling, that is, his covenant. In simple terms, the man and the woman completely trust God. They are "nakedly" innocent of all knowledge of evil (v. 5).

But found within the serpent's life-altering interplay, deception's plate is offered up. The creature subtly proclaims that if the couple would but take

---

1. See NET, study note "n," Gen 3:5.
2. See Arnold, *Genesis*, 66.
3. See Walton, *Lost World of Adam and Eve*, 143.

and eat the forbidden fruit, they too would become *God-like* in their knowing, which includes the full palate between "good and evil."[4] Kenton Sparks elaborates, "Humanity harbors in its heart a misplaced desire for divine knowledge and prerogative."[5] Further, this status confers "life," evident in the serpent's phrasing, "Surely you will not die." In short, the serpent offers an entirely new paradigm for viewing and living life. There is a downside, however, to what is being offered. To attain such "God-like status" the human couple must abandon the Creator. This, then, is the danger inherent in the temptation of the fruit. As for the woman who plucks the tree's fruit ("took some" = ethical choice), she concedes to the serpent that its deceptive version of "truth" is best. As the couple bites deeply into the forbidden fruit, Yahweh's covenant for living sours in their mouths. They have been turned.

Microstructure: Yahweh Confronts the Man and the Woman

In contrast to the serpent (who is immediately tried), Yahweh confronts the man and woman with truth-questions. The seriousness of what they did is heard as God, now the Investigator, asks, "Where are you?" The Creator, of course, has no interest in literally knowing where they are; obviously he knows their location. The question is rhetorical. They are faced with the knowledge that *wherever they are*, their friend Yahweh *is not there*. This meaning is reinforced by God's second question, "Who told you that you were naked?" Again, God knows the answer. He asks it solely to inform the couple of their now-altered life paradigm, indicated by the word "naked" (3:7).

The word "naked" occurs three times in the garden scene. Here, the number *three* is a callback; it reminds ancient readers of the sacred image in which the man and the woman were created. As sacred beings, their choice to eat the banned fruit distanced themselves from God. Having broken the Creator's covenant, indicated by their now-ashamed and naked condition, the man and the woman are, in effect, dwelling outside the boundaries of sacred living. Tragically, whatever remains of their authority to "rule" will be at best shaky, a vile mix of evil and good. Here, then, is the genesis of a dark downfall, a trail of tears and tragedy that will blot their capacity to rule well and wisely as God's overseers of his good creation. They no longer

---

4. See NET, study note "n," Gen 3:5.
5. Sparks, "Genesis 1–11 as Ancient Historiography," 124.

hold God's lifeview, his paradigm for wise living. The fall of human rule has commenced.

To recap the events in the garden so far, we turn to John, author of the New Testament letter that Christians label First John. In it, John follows the early chapters of Genesis, and so he writes, "That which was from the *beginning* . . ." (emphasis added). In chapter 2 (vv. 15–17), John continues with Genesis in view, "For everything in the *world*—the lust of the flesh, the lust of the eyes, and the pride of life—comes not from the Father but from the *world*" (emphasis added). John's statement, which addresses the contrariness of the world's point of view is lifted directly from Gen 3:6: "When the woman saw that the fruit of the tree was good for food and pleasing to the eye, and also desirable for gaining wisdom . . ." The point of this comparison is that John saw the events in the garden not so much as "sin," "rebellion," or "transgression" as he did an exchange *from* trust in God *to* reliance on the "world," which is the serpent's paradigm for living.

By calling what happened to the man and the woman "sin" or "the fall," many Christians have sought an easier path to explain the garden events. In other words, if something can be labeled, it can be explained without regard to thought. But mere labeling does not make for critical explanations.[6] Just saying that Adam and Eve "sinned"—and therefore making the connection "that all have sinned"—is a failure to look at what the Genesis text is saying. Nowhere in Gen 3 does the biblical author use the word "sin,"[7] nor is the drama presented as premeditated rebellion.

Walter Brueggemann takes up the question of the "fall" in his discussion on Gen 3. In a general statement he sets the tone for his remarks: "No text in Genesis (or likely the entire Bible) has been more used, interpreted, and misunderstood than this text"[8] (referring to all of 2:4b—3:24, with specific focus on the serpent and Eve). Rejecting the idea that this passage is "a decisive text for the Bible," he says of the "fall" that "nothing could be more remote from the narrative itself."[9] Brueggemann adds, "The Old Testament does not assume such a 'fall.'"[10] Indeed, John Walton writes similarly but

---

6. Moberly, writing within a "wisdom" context, offers "life and sacred texts are more complex and problematic than initially seemed to be the case." Moberly, *Theology of Genesis*, 87.

7. The interpretation that this event heralds sin largely occurs within a New Testament context, as it reinterprets the Genesis "fall."

8. Brueggemann, *Genesis*, 41.

9. Brueggemann, *Genesis*, 41.

10. Brueggemann, *Genesis*, 41.

from ancient culture's view. Walton claims, "The Old Testament never refers to the event of Genesis 3 as 'the fall' and does not talk about people or the world as 'fallen.'"[11]

This view, then, establishes an altered paradigm when set against accepted orthodoxy, which my be simplified as *"original sin."* The real "sin" of the garden, however, was the lost opportunity to gain (or continue to hold) access to God[12] (through the figurative tree of life) and move beyond human mortality.[13] The events in the garden indicate that some believers have failed to adequately understand the basic problem of humanity. The fundamental and core issue with the race is not that we "sinned" in the garden but that we exchanged *God's lifeview*, or in the minds of some theologians, wisdom, that went with being created in the image of God.[14] It was that view which knew only God and his goodness. It was a view that knew nothing of sin, evil, and darkness. But humanity's unadulterated and "naked" view (Gen 2:25), formed out of pure innocence, was lost when the man and the woman took and ate the fruit. By doing so, they made an ethical choice. God, in his wisdom, did not desire for humanity to know evil while they were still mortal beings.[15] His intent was for them to know only goodness. As the Lord of Creation, God is aware that humanity offers evil, represented by the symbol word "serpent," opportunity to reign through a now-fallen-from-goodness race.[16] An evil, as Jon Levenson writes, that in its malignancy "opposes everything he [God] is reputed to uphold."[17]

The test in the garden, then, was a test of entrustment: trust God's knowledge (i.e., his wisdom) or trust the serpent (i.e., his lies). That test question—who is to be believed, God or the serpent—humanity failed. And with it came the knowledge of evil, a distortion that ever since has plagued humanity in its role as rulers over the created order. What was lost in the "fall" was the race's capacity to rule for "good." It is not that humans can't be good, but the concept of good and ability to be good were stolen

---

11. Walton, *Lost World of Adam and Eve*, 142.

12. Walton, *Lost World of Adam and Eve*, 145.

13. Walton, *Lost World of Adam and Eve*, Proposition 8 (73) and Proposition 15 (144–45). Hence, "Besides the likelihood that Genesis 3:19 suggests people were created mortal" (73) and "Their failure meant that we are doomed to death and a disordered world full of sin" (145). See also James Barr, *Garden of Eden and the Hope of Immortality*.

14. See Walton, *Lost World of Adam and Eve*, 142–45.

15. See for example, Barr, *Garden of Eden and the Hope of Immortality*.

16. Averbeck, "Ancient Near Eastern Mythography," 354.

17. Levenson, *Persistence of Evil*, xxiii.

away when humans adopted the serpent's paradigm for living, which the apostle John considers a *"worldview"*[18] (1 John 2:15–16). This is now a race that no longer can rule in the expected fullness of beings created in the image of God. This altered condition leads to the segment's peak moment, and with it comes the question, What will Yahweh do about a race that is suddenly *naked and ashamed*? (3:10–11).

Second Scene: Overview of the Courtroom Scene

The importance of structure as a literary device to enhance textual meaning is artfully presented in the courtroom segment through poetry. Often, Bible publishers highlight the scene's three poetic judgments by setting them into stylistic prominence, such as through italics or centering the text rather than using left justification.[19] Hence, for readers, the text presents as a visual signal, but for ancient listeners, the text echoes a poetic cadence. By that auditory means, a reader (more likely a listener) is invited to recall the number of times the ancient writer used poetry in the creation narratives. That callback count reveals this is the *third* time the biblical author has narrated in poetry. Not only is it the third time, but the poem too is set within a *triadic* structure (i.e., the serpent on trial, the woman on trial, the man on trial).

Such doubling down recalls the first time the author employed poetry, which occurred in context with the creation of humanity (1:27). It was at that point in the creation story that the Hebrew word *bara* (created) occurred in a tight, threefold cluster. Through this parallel correspondence, used now in the courtroom scene and prior in the creation of humanity, the biblical author presents a most apparent fact. That is, it is God, not the serpent, who is the Sovereign Creator. It is God who created the man and the woman in his sacred image, a rulership image based in goodness, and not in the image of the serpent who is depicted as a slinky, wild, and chaos-inducing creature. Therefore, the full right to invest the man and the woman with the divine perspective falls to God[20] alone. It is God's right to

---

18. Moberly considers the garden story to be a form of wisdom literature. See Moberly, *Theology of God*, 87.

19. C. John Collins finds this scene to be the passage's peak. The importance of that to the author's message will be shortly determined. Collins, *Genesis 1–4*, 168.

20. Moberly writes of God, "knows what is best for them." This comes within an alternative examination of the "fall" story. See Moberly, *Theology of Genesis*, 79, which is set within 78–83.

expect from the human couple obedience as they move about in his sacred garden. Accordingly, the man and the woman are under an ethical obligation to obey God's injunctions regarding the banned fruit.

Microstructure in the Second Scene: The Serpent on Trial

Significantly, God first sentences the serpent. That act comes without the benefit of an investigation (see vv. 9–13). Thus, God's graciousness is not extended to the "wild animal." It is here that the word "curse" is first used in Scripture. This word may mean "punished" or "banished."[21] As used here, it likely carries both meanings since the serpent is simultaneously punished and banished. God's sentencing of the serpent seems bent on bringing down the creature's lofty status, that is, its immense ego as head of the wild animals. Here, we must recognize that the judgment poem, as with the story, is more allegorical than historical, more mythical than actual. Longman affirms this, stating, "The writer does not intend the reader to take the description of creation of the cosmos or of humanity as literally true."[22] Thus, in the garden judgment, humanity falls short of gaining life eternal (or continuing to live without dying).[23] Yet its scope ranges far beyond the reality of one moment in (representational) human history. After all, the word *adam* means "human" and "Eve" refers to "life."

What looms behind the serpent's figuration as a wild animal, though, is the church's tradition of Satan. Thus, the text declares that this creature will "eat dust all the days of your life." As the NET notes, eating dust symbolizes humility,[24] perhaps the harshest sentence that could be imposed on this arrogant "wild animal," since its desire is *to rule* (i.e., be like God) and be worshiped (i.e., as if God). Those attributes—rulership and worship—were the motivational snares behind the serpent's attack on the couple, and they reveal the serpent's intent for launching this assault on humanity. Speaking canonically (in the Christian tradition), the serpent saw in this new race the potential to gain what it desired, namely, to replace God and become the object of worship. In parallel actions, human rulers often copycat the serpent's paranoia, seeking to puff themselves up, often by lies, boasts, and

---

21. NET, translator note "ak," Gen 3:14.

22. Longman, "What Genesis 1–2 Teaches (and Doesn't)," 104.

23. This is, according to Moberly's reading, James Barr's position. Moberly, *Theology of Genesis*, 75.

24. NET, study note "am," Gen 3:14.

outrageous claims filled with arrogant deception. Employing that strategy, they seek from their followers the status of godlikeness. Tragically, too many of today's political and religious leaders have wandered deeply into deception, casting themselves as heroic, cultic figures and their followers in the role of cultic worshipers.

Adding to the creature's sentencing, God announces a great hostility within humanity, which entails the race's own alienation. Hereafter there will be two sides to humankind: one comprised of those who follow the power-seeking serpent (i.e., holders of the serpent's worldview), while the other side clings to God (and his lifeview). These two oppositional sides will perpetually collide.

The text forecasts a future battleground based on this division.[25] It will be fought upon a landscape of two opposing outlooks, the outcome of which will be determined by two champions in a distant and undisclosed future time (3:15). As to that outcome, both will suffer. The head of the serpent's champion will be "bruised," that is, "crushed." While most interpret this as a mortal blow, the context here, given the humiliation and denial of what the serpent fomented—that is, a desire to be worshiped and to rule—likely suggests that this blow to the head ends all chances that the creature's dysfunctional psyche will ever gain its end.

As for the woman's offspring, he too will suffer grievously. By continuing to follow the metaphor of a serpent (snake) crawling on its belly, this likely alludes to how the serpent attacks its victim, by heel-biting. As with the bite of any poisonous reptile, the creature's venom carries potential for death. In the Christian tradition, this battleground anticipates the cross on which Christ would die for all of Eve's children—indeed, for all of humanity (John 3:16).

Microstructure: The Woman on Trial

Leaving the serpent, God turns to the woman. In doing so, we must be careful to avoid contemporary "culture wars" that might affect our reading of the text. The woman's punishment is twofold and coincides with her

---

25. That division and a final battle may be framed in the book of Revelation as composed of two types of "casts." One is the cast of characters that sides with God's "the Lamb and the Lion," while the other aligns with the Serpent now transformed into the "Dragon/Devil." For presenting the book of Revelation around a "cast of characters," I am indebted to Dr. Corey Johnsrud, sermon, Jul. 6, 2025.

exalted role as giver of life. This is first depicted as sentencing falls upon her through motherhood. The text reads, "I will make your pains in childbearing very severe." But in the repeated line, "with painful labor you will give birth to children," is the idea that this "pain" ranges beyond just the moment of birth and extends to the pain (i.e., worry, fear, heartache) which comes to mothers over the lifespan of their children.[26]

The woman's second punishment is found in the poem's last line. The NIV renders, "Your desire will be for your husband, and he will rule over you." Two words must be considered: "desire" and "rule." "Desire" was previously used in verse 6 ("and also desirable for gaining wisdom"). This word connection suggests that the biblical author is directing attention to that which separated the woman from the man. Hence, the author adds the phrase "for gaining wisdom." The woman's error, then, was the misplacement of her desire. First, she chose not to discuss the "temptation" with her husband but rather heed the serpent's counsel ("For God knows that when you eat from it your eyes will be opened," v. 5). Part of her desire was the temptation to rule on her own, to no longer be co-joined with her husband. Hence, her single-mindedness wedged apart the couple's unity, contrary to the intent of the marriage metaphor (2:24, "become one flesh"). In other words, the more she sought the fruit which granted wisdom, the more she moved toward isolation, alienation, and disunification.

With that in mind, the last part of the woman's punishment becomes clearer, which is the husband's rule over her. By declaring that the husband is to "rule over" her, the biblical author returns to the woman's creation, described in 1:26 and 1:28, namely as co-ruler over the created order. Thus, reference to the man's rule is intended to reorient the woman to God's purpose for the two genders, which is the man and the woman acting together,[27] signaled by the text's symbolic use of marriage. Here, God's judgment finds its locus in restorative mercy rather than harsh servitude under an equally unprepared *adam*.

Microstructure: The Man on Trial

God's judgment of the man occurs in two contexts. The first is heard, "Because you listened to your wife" (v. 17). The NET translates "listened" as "obeyed." It adds in a footnote, explaining "listened to your wife" as a

---

26. NET, study note "am," Gen 3:14.
27. See Middleton, *Liberating Image*, 206.

language expression meaning to "obey."[28] Thus, the man elected to "obey" the voice of his wife rather than the voice of God. In this case, the man's role as co-ruler was weakened by his silent complicity, his failure to speak out as the woman was dragged down by the serpent. Indeed, he voided the rulership conferred upon him by God as he failed to rule through wisdom; he failed to keep safe not only the garden but the most sacred gift given to him, the woman God made as a blessing for him. If he had acted to keep Eve safe, he would have intervened when the serpent abused her with questions.

The second judgment context is rooted in a Hebrew wordplay since the word for "ground" is *adamah*. Similarly, we must recall that Adam's name in Hebrew (which is *adam*) means "humanity." Thus, these two similar-sounding Hebrew words link the man Adam to the ground out of which he was created. We first heard this connection in 2:7, as the text states, "Then the Lord God formed a man ('*adam*') from the dust of the ground ('*adamah*')..." Now, in the man's punishment, the biblical author again uses this repetition of Hebrew sounds to recall the association between Adam's name and ground.

With that word association in mind, we are prepared to comprehend God's verdict. The Creator sentences the man, stating, "*Cursed is the ground* because of you" (3:17; emphasis added). It is at this point that we recall God's six-day work in the first creation story. In that work, described through two three-day panels, Elohim first prepared *adamah* ("ground") *as sacred space*. Further, *adam* (humanity) was created within the *sacred image of God on the sixth day*. Now we find God placing a "*curse*" not upon Adam but his namesake, *adamah* (the ground). In other words, the author indicates that "*adamah*/ground" will bear the curse/punishment for "*adam*/human."

In theological terms this sounds very much like a form of substitution in which the ground takes the place of Adam, bearing the consequential curse for disobedience. (See Gal 3:10–14, "Christ redeemed us from the curse of the law by becoming a curse for us.") While at this time in the meta-story of God's unconditional love, the full understanding of Christ as redemptive sacrifice for humanity is not in view, yet within the full range of Scripture's meta-story, of which Gen 1–11 sits as prologue, the seeds are laid for the coming of "*the suffering servant*."[29]

---

28. NET, translator note "az" in 3:17.
29. See Jer 52:13—53:12

Tragically, the man and the woman, who lost their bid to gain immortality,[30] now, in a kind of poetic justice, find the *ground's dust* becoming their final resting place. The biblical writer states, "For out of it you were taken; for you are dust, and to dust you will return." And so *adam* returns to *adamah*; dust to dust and ground to ground, the unsacred to the sacred, all of which adds to the plot line going forward. As prologue, Gen 1–11 ramps up the question of how God will restore the race of *adam* and the sacred ground *adamah* to "goodness."

Having worked through the triadic courtroom judgment, we are now able to discern why the second judgement, that of the woman, is the garden story's theological peak.[31] The segment's triadic structure (see figure 28), with its two judgment bases—the *curse* on the serpent (3:14–15) and the *curse* on the ground of which humanity will return to its dust (3:17–19)—*both orient to death*. It is only in the woman's sentencing that *the text speaks to life*,[32] indicated by the woman's name.

FIGURE 28. GARDEN JUDGMENT AND CURSE

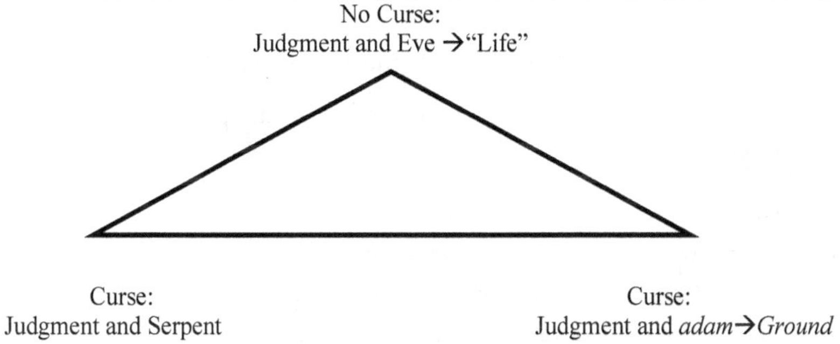

No Curse:
Judgment and Eve →"Life"

Curse:
Judgment and Serpent

Curse:
Judgment and *adam*→*Ground*

Despite the text's bent toward life, the rejection of God's covenant in the "garden fall," compounded by the corruption of the image in which humanity was created, will combine to haunt the race throughout the rest of its history. A critical review of that future finds it is filled with indictments of cruelty and violence; further, the race is stamped as one alienated from God and fragmented within itself rather than one holding a human/divine relationship graced with honor and goodness. If we wonder how a species

---

30. See Cassuto, *Commentary on Genesis*, 125.
31. Collins, *Genesis 1-4*, 168.
32. See Brueggmann, *Genesis*, 42, subsection "d."

so endowed with intelligence and goodness can act so harmfully, preying upon one another as wild animals might, here are its seeds, seeds which even today, thousands of years later, continue to flower into a never-ending, thorn-filled bouquet of outrageous and horrific acts.

Therefore—as passage peak—it is the woman's consequence that shapes the creation narrative going forward. It prefigures the biblical theme of life over death and light over darkness, yet humanity's long journey will experience Eve's pain (3:16) through continual conflict. However, what is most important is the question of Yahweh's intent. The storyline asks, What will become of God's desire to construct a sacred temple now that his image-bearers have been despoiled? How will rule over God's creation be carried out in goodness, and who will serve God in that capacity?

Third Scene: Expulsion

Four things happen in the final segment.

1. The woman is named Eve (v. 20).
2. God clothes the couple (v. 21).
3. The text explains why the couple must be expelled (v. 22).
4. Upon expulsion, cherubim are placed as border guards on the eastern edge of the garden (v. 24).

The above story outline ends Adam and Eve's time in the garden. By naming the woman "Eve,"[33] the writer signals the narrative intent of the text. It is a declaration that the creation of life, spotlighted through Eve's name, is the central interest of God. Further, by God clothing the couple, the text indicates the need for the now-naked and ashamed human race to be re-clothed, properly "dressed" for a renewed relationship with God. More so, by God's rejecting the couple's outfitting of themselves with fig leaves, notice is given that God alone can transform humanity from its now-naked and ashamed status to its original creation condition of naked innocence. In the New Testament tradition, this act is given over to God alone, a teaching that is presented, for example, in Christ's parables on wedding garments.[34]

---

33. The significance of naming the woman at this point in the story and not prior, when it would be more convenient for readers, must not be missed.

34. See Matt 22:1–14, with emphasis on vv. 11–13.

The third point, expulsion, has to do with the inherent danger of continuing to live in the garden. If the man and the woman should reach out and eat from the tree of life in their present condition—which is their radicalized worldview of trusting the serpent—they would forever live under the serpent's evil rule. In the end, God had to expel them. By posting an angelic sentry, God removed the task formerly assigned to the man and the woman. What was left for them was "to work the ground"[35] outside of the garden's boundaries. And with that, Adam and Eve's time in the garden of Eden closes but not the story of beginnings.

It is therefore significant what we hear from Yahweh through his final spoken words. "The man has now become like one of us, knowing good and evil. He must not be allowed to reach out his hand and take also from the tree of life and eat, and live forever" (v. 22). In a like manner, the narrator ends this passage writing, "After he drove the man out, he placed on the east side of the Garden of Eden cherubim and a flaming sword flashing back and forth to guard the way to the tree of life." Thus, in both instances the final words find focus not on death but life. This deliberate symmetry of thought indicates that in this story of humanity, though the race seemingly has abandoned God, God has not abandoned his image-bearers.

How the story turns out, as Adam and Eve are driven from the garden and begin the long walk toward an eastern horizon, will be resumed in the second book of this series.

SUMMARY

In this unit, the importance of reading the garden story from the literary genre of theology and myth was illustrated. Further, attention to structure and micro-structure added additional interpretive detail. By following the story's three scenes, we were able to see how the biblical writer presented certain truth-claims. Among them was this question, Which paradigm for living will ancient Israel adopt? Will Israel conform to the worldview of the serpent, filled with deception, distortion, and lies? Or will Israel take-up Yahweh's lifeview, centered upon truth, goodness, and godliness? In the end, the story of the "fall" is a story of ethical choice. And with the human couple's decision comes a blockage preventing access to God and the sacred garden site. All of which renders the story's most crucial question, How will the Creator respond to humanity, now naked and ashamed? More so, if

---

35. See Alexander, *From Eden*, 26.

God elects to re-engage with Adam and Eve's race, what will that response cost (him)?

CONCLUSION TO UNIT 2 AND BOOK 1

Unit 2, in comparison to Unit 1, reveals a second creation story. However, despite differences in story content, there exists between Gen 1 and 2 a distinct unification. The Genesis author's continued use of literary structure is one feature binding these chapters together. Another is the theme of human rulership.

Through literary elements such as these, the two distinct creation stories are drawn together, united under one coherent theological narrative, of which human rulership is one of several themes. Of particular importance is how the formation of the woman drives the text's theological meaning. This is understood as the text suddenly pivots to marriage-like language, declaring, "It is not good for the man to be alone," followed by "a man will leave his father and mother and be united to his wife, and they will become one flesh." The salient point of these statements lies not in the institution of matrimony but rather in the unification of the two genders as one (faith community). The importance of that unification is discovered when the serpent enters the paradise garden. Alarmingly, the bond that unites the man and the woman in Gen 2 is fractured in Gen 3. Even more egregiously, as Adam and Eve head eastward, with each step forward they become more spatially distanced from their Maker.

Overall, then, Genesis's two units tell a narrative in which Adam and Eve were given the important task of sustaining earth's artfully designed habitat and caring for all of God's creatures. In a simplified way, that's what to be made in God's image entails. Reduced to one word, which is drawn from Gen 1 and Gen 2, humanity is to conduct its commissioned rule frocked in "goodness."

Gen 1 and 2 saw the rise of human rule[36] and how humanity was to conduct caretaking in alliance with the Creator. But a specter of conflict, like darkness over the primordial sea, looms over the narrative. It arrives in the telling of Gen 3's drama involving the garden's fruit trees. Electing to depart from God's lifeview, the race "fell" through disobedience by not trusting God's covenant mandate. It was in the human couple's disobedience that allegiance was transferred from God to the serpent as the man

36. Middleton, *Liberating Image*, 212.

and the woman accepted the worldview flowing from chaos and evil. The story of that "falling out," therefore, forms the content of Gen 4–11.

Beyond Myth Conclusion

As this book closes the creation story of Gen 1–3, today's readers are left with the task of formulating a biblical response to the church's twenty-first century abandonment of God's lifeview. Jumping from ancient times to today's world, arguably a large segment of the church has been swept up in the same type of chaotic deception that "fell" Adam and Eve. And with it, the church's ability to rule well and for the good of others has been greatly impaired.

In this book's preface, mention was made of a biblical plumb line, thereby suggesting a standard by which human rule could be assessed and informed. That plumb line consists of the many attributes uncovered in this examination of rulership, all of which may be subsumed under goodness. When "goodness" is applied as an outcome test question to the church's current drift into the murky world of political alliances, there is more than sufficient reason to conclude that a large segment of the ecclesia has, like the human couple in the garden, taken a deep dive into chaos, deception, and Christian nationalism.

The results are evident in the fragmentation of the church.[37] Like Adam and Eve, the church is no longer (if it ever was) "naked and innocent." Its fig-like coverings are insufficient to cover and hide the downward spiral to chaos. And yet, as the text preserved hope for Adam and Eve, so too is hope maintained for the race's sacred commission to rule well. That pathway, metaphorically pictured in the "marriage" text's emphasis on oneness and unity, is described in optimistic detail in Skyler Flowers and Michael Graham's insightful essay, in which they write, "For the evangelical movement to remain a movement motivated by the spread of the gospel and the glory of God, it must embrace an evangelical catholicity."[38] Yet, that "catholicity" must be forged along different lines than in the past. And, as was the case with Adam and Eve who no longer found themselves dwelling safely in the garden, so too must the church reorient itself to a new geography of relationships, abandoning the politics of division, and move toward a broader

---

37. Flowers and Graham categorize this fragmentation into seven splinters. See Flowers and Graham, "Splintered Generation," 38.

38. Flowers and Graham, "Splintered Generation," 45.

acceptance in which there is room and respect to be different yet united within the metaphorical picture of a marital oneness (2:24). How that plays out for the race in antiquity forms the content of the second volume in this series; how that works for today's ecclesia remains yet an unanswered question.

Bibliography

Abernethy, Andrew T., ed. *Interpreting the Old Testament Theologically*. Grand Rapids: Zondervan, 2018.
Alexander, Desmond T. *From Eden to the New Jerusalem: An Introduction to Biblical Theology*. Grand Rapids: Kregel, 2008.
———. *From Paradise to the Promised Land: An Introduction to the Pentateuch*. 3rd ed. Grand Rapids: Kregel, 2012.
Anderson, Bernhard W. *Creation Versus Chaos: The Reinterpretation of Mythical Symbolism in the Bible*. Eugene, OR: Wipf & Stock, 1987.
Arnold, Bill T., ed. *The Cambridge Companion to Genesis*. Cambridge, UK: Cambridge University Press, 2022.
———. *Genesis*. New Cambridge Bible Commentary. New York: Cambridge University Press, 2009.
Atkinson, David. *The Message of Genesis 1–11: The Dawn of Creation*. Downers Grove, IL: InterVarsity, 1990.
Averbeck, Richard E. "Ancient Near Eastern Mythography as It Relates to Historiography in the Hebrew Bible: Genesis 3 and the Cosmic Battle." In *The Future of Biblical Archaeology*, edited by James K. Hoffmeier, 328–56. Grand Rapids: Eerdmans, 2004.
———. "A Literary Day, Inter-Textual, and Contextual Reading of Genesis 1–2." In *Reading Genesis 1–2: An Evangelical Conversation*, edited by Daryl Charles, 7–32. Peabody, MA: Hendrickson, 2013.
Barclay, William. *The Letter to the Hebrews*. Revised ed. Philadelphia: Westminster Press, 1976.
Barr, James. *The Garden of Eden and the Hope of Immortality*. London: SCM, 1992.
Beal, Todd S. "Reading Genesis 1–2: A Literal Approach." In *Reading Genesis 1–2: An Evangelical Conversation*, edited by Daryl Charles, 45–59. Peabody, MA: Hendrickson, 2013.
Bible Translation Committee, "Introduction to the New Living Translation." New Living Translation, A11–17.
Blenkinsopp, Joseph. *Creation, Un-Creation, Re-Creation: A Discursive Commentary on Genesis 1–11*. New York: Clark, 2011.
Bloesch, Donald G. *Holy Scripture: Revelation, Inspiration and Interpretation*. Downers Grove, IL: InterVarsity, 1994.
Bouteneff, Peter C. *Beginnings: Ancient Christian Readings of the Biblical Creation Narratives*. Grand Rapids: Baker, 2008.

Bibliography

Boyd, Gregory A. "Christus Victor View." In *The Nature of Atonement: Four Views*, edited by James Beilby and Paul R. Eddy. Downers Grove, IL: InterVarsity, 2006.

Brayford, Susan. *Genesis*. Septuagint Commentary. Boston: Brill, 2007.

Brodie, Thomas, L. *Genesis as Dialogue: A Literary, Historical, and Theological Commentary*. New York: Oxford University Press, 2001.

Brueggemann, Walter. *Genesis: Interpretation A Bible Commentary for Teaching and Preaching*. Atlanta: John Knox, 1982.

Cassuto, Umberto. *A Commentary on the Book of Genesis*. Jerusalem: Hebrew University Magnes, 1961.

Charles, Daryl J., ed. *Reading Genesis 1-2: An Evangelical Conversation*. Peabody, MA: Hendrickson, 2013.

Coleson, Joseph. *Genesis 1-11: A Commentary in the Wesleyan Tradition*. Kansas City, KS: Beacon Hill, 2012.

Collins, C. John. *Genesis 1-4: A Linguistic, Literary, and Theological Commentary*. Phillipsburg, NJ: P&R, 2006.

———. "Reading Genesis 1-2 With The Grain: Analogical Days." In *Reading Genesis 1-2: An Evangelical Conversation*, edited by Daryl Charles, 73–92. Peabody, MA: Hendrickson, 2013.

Conn, Harvey M., ed. *Inerrancy and Hermeneutic: A Tradition, a Challenge, a Debate*. Grand Rapids: Baker, 1988.

Cross, Frank Moore. *Canaanite Myth and Hebrew Epic: Essays in the History of the Religion of Israel*. Cambridge, MA: Harvard University Press, 1973.

Davis, Jud. "Unresolved Major Questions: Evangelicals and Genesis 1-2." In *Reading Genesis 1-2: An Evangelical Conversation*, edited by Daryl Charles, 207–31. Peabody, MA: Hendrickson, 2013.

Dempster, Stephen G. *Dominion and Dynasty: A Theology of the Hebrew Bible*. Madison, WI: InterVarsity, 2003.

Dorsey, David A. *The Literary Structure of the Old Testament: A Commentary on Genesis-Malachi*. Grand Rapids: Baker, 1999.

Du Mez, Kristin Kobes. *Jesus and John Wayne: How White Evangelicals Corrupted a Faith and Fractured a Nation*. New York: Liveright, 2020.

Durkee, Alison. "Dominion Defamation Case." *Forbes*, Apr. 18, 2023. https://www.forbes.com/sites/alisondurkee/2023/04/18/fox-news-settles-dominion-defamation-case-for-7875-million-dominion-lawyer-says/.

Eberhart, Christian. *The Sacrifice of Jesus: Understanding Atonement Biblically*. Minneapolis: Fortress, 2011.

Fleming, Daniel E. "Genesis in History and Tradition: The Syrian Background of Israel's Ancestors, Reprise." In *The Future of Biblical Archaeology: Reassessing Methodologies and Assumptions*, edited by James K. Hoffmeier and Alan Millard, 193–232. Grand Rapids: Eerdmans, 2004.

Flowers, Skyler R., and Michael Graham. "A Splintered Generation." *Christianity Today*, May/Jun. 2025, 36–45.

Garner, Paul. *The New Creationism: Building Scientific Theories on a Biblical Foundation*. Welwyn Garden City, UK: EP, 2009.

Graves, Robert, and Raphael Patai. *Hebrew Myths: The Book of Genesis*. Garden City, NY: Doubleday, 1964.

Habel, Norman. *Literary Criticism of the Old Testament*. Philadelphia: Fortress, 1971.

Bibliography

Haidt, Jonathan. "Why the Past 10 Years of American Life Have Been Uniquely Stupid." *The Atlantic*, May 2022, 54–66.

Halton, Charles, and Stanley N. Gundry, eds. *Genesis: History, Fiction, or Neither?: Three Views on the Bible's Earliest Chapters*. Grand Rapids: Zondervan, 2015.

Hamilton, Victor P. *The Book of Genesis, Chapters 1–17*. Grand Rapids: Eerdmans, 1990.

Hays, Richard B. *Reading Backwards: Figural Christology and the Fourfold Gospel Witness*. Waco, TX: Baylor University Press, 2014.

Heidel, Alexander. *The Babylonian Genesis*. Chicago: University of Chicago Press, 1942.

Hendel, Ronald. *The Book of Genesis: A Biography*. Princeton, NJ: Princeton University Press, 2013.

Hoffmeier, James K., and Alan Millard, eds. *The Future of Biblical Archaeology: Reassessing Methodologies and Assumptions*. Grand Rapids: Eerdmans, 2004.

———. "Genesis 1–11 as History and Theology." In *Genesis: History, Fiction, or Neither*, edited by Charles Halton and Stanley N. Gundry, 23–58. Grand Rapids: Zondervan, 2015.

Kapur, Sahil, et al. "Republicans Block Independent Commission to Investigate Attack on U.S. Capitol." NBC News, May 28, 2021. https://www.nbcnews.com/politics/congress/was-attack-our-capitol-murkowski-criticizes-gop-colleagues-opposing-jan-n1268906.

Kikiwada, Isaac M., and Arthur Quinn. *Before Abraham Was: A Provocative Challenge to the Documentary Hypothesis*. Nashville: Abingdon, 1985.

Kline, Meredith G. *Kingdom Prologue: Genesis Foundations for a Covenantal Worldview*. Eugene, OR: Wipf & Stock, 2006.

Kugel, James L. *The Bible as It Was*. Cambridge, MA: Harvard University Press, 1997.

Lamoureux, Denis O. *The Bible and Ancient Science: Principles of Interpretation*. Tullahoma, TN: McGahan, 2020.

Levenson, Jon D. *Creation and the Persistence of Evil: The Jewish Drama of Divine Omnipotence*. Princeton, NJ: Princeton University Press, 1988.

Lindsell, Harold. *Battle for the Bible*. Grand Rapids: Zondervan, 1976.

Longman, Tremper, III. "Storytellers and Poets in the Bible: Can Literary Artifice Be True?" In *Inerrancy and Hermeneutic: A Tradition, a Challenge, a Debate*, edited by Harvie M. Conn, 137–49. Grand Rapids: Baker, 1988.

———. "What Genesis 1–2 Teaches (and What It Doesn't)." In *Reading Genesis 1–2: An Evangelical Conversation*, edited by Daryl Charles, 103–26. Peabody, MA: Hendrickson, 2013.

———., and Raymond B. Dillard. *An Introduction to the Old Testament*. 2nd ed. Grand Rapids: Zondervan, 2006.

———., and John H. Walton. *The Lost Word of the Flood: Mythology, Theology, and the Deluge Debate*. Downers Grove, IL: IVP, 2018.

Louth, Andrew, and Thomas C. Oden, eds. *Genesis 1–11*. Ancient Christian Commentary on Scripture: Old Testament I. Downers Grove, IL: InterVarsity, 2001.

Matthews, Kenneth A. *Genesis 1–11:26*. New American Commentary: An Exegetical and Theological Exposition of Holy Scripture. Nashville: Broadman & Homan, 1996.

Metzger, Bruce. *Breaking the Code: Understanding the Book of Revelation*. Nashville: Abingdon, 2019.

Middleton, J. Richard. *The Liberating Image: The Imago Dei in Genesis 1*. Grand Rapids: Brazos, 2005.

Milgrom, Jacob. *Leviticus*. Minneapolis: Fortress, 2004.

Bibliography

Miller, Johnny V., and John M. Soden. *In the Beginning . . . We Misunderstood*. Grand Rapids: Kregel, 2012.

Moberly, R. W. L. *The Theology of the Book of Genesis*. New York: Cambridge University Press, 2009.

Monson, John. "Original Context and Canon." In *Interpreting the Old Testament Theologically*, edited by Andrew Abernethy, 25–42. Grand Rapids: Zondervan, 2018.

———. "The Role of Context and the Promise of Archaeology in Biblical Interpretation from Early Judaism to Post Modernity." In *The Future of Biblical Archaeology*, edited by James K. Hoffmeier, 309–27. Grand Rapids: Eerdmans, 2004.

Moore, Russell. "Losing Our Taste for the Fruit of the Spirit." *Christianity Today*, Nov. 2022, 34.

———. "Mount Zion or Mar-a-Lago." *Christianity Today*, Jul./Aug. 2024, 19–21.

New World Encyclopedia. "Enuma Elish." https://www.newworldencyclopedia.org/entry/Enuma_Elish.

Reno, R. R. *Genesis*. Grand Rapids: Brazos, 2010.

Robertson, Pat (host). *The 700 Club*. Episode aired on CBN, May 29, 2021.

Rose Book of Bible Charts, Maps, and Time Lines. Torrance, CA: Rose, 2005.

Sailhamer, John H. *Genesis Unbounded: A Provocative New Look at the Creation Account*. 2nd ed. Colorado Springs, CO: Book Villages, 2011.

———. *The Pentateuch as Narrative: A Biblical-Theological Commentary*. Grand Rapids: Zondervan, 1992.

Schaeffer, Francis A. *Genesis in Space and Time: The Flow of Biblical History*. Downers Grove, IL: InterVarsity, 1972.

Schreiner, Thomas R. *The King in His Beauty: A Biblical Theology of the Old and New Testaments*. Grand Rapids: Baker, 2013.

Schroeder, Joy A. *The Book of Genesis: The Bible in Medieval Tradition*. Grand Rapids: Eerdmans, 2015.

Silva, Moises. *Has the Church Misread the Bible? The History of Interpretation in the Light of Current Issues*. Grand Rapids: Zondervan Academic, 1987.

Ska, Jean-Louis. "Genesis in the History of Critical Scholarship." In *The Cambridge Companion to Genesis*, edited by Bill Arnold, 11–52. Cambridge, UK: Cambridge University Press, 2022.

Sparks, Kenton L. "Genesis 1–11 as Ancient Historiography." In *Genesis: History, Fiction, or Neither?: Three Views on the Bible's Earliest Chapters*, edited by Charles Halton and Stanley N. Gundry, 110–39. Grand Rapids: Zondervan, 2015.

———. "Response to Gordon J. Wenham." In *Genesis: History, Fiction, or Neither?: Three Views on the Bible's Earliest Chapters*, edited by Charles Halton and Stanley N. Gundry, 101–9. Grand Rapids: Zondervan, 2015.

———. "Response to James K. Hoffmeier." In *Genesis: History, Fiction, or Neither?: Three Views on the Bible's Earliest Chapters*, edited by Charles Halton and Stanley N. Gundry, 63–72. Grand Rapids: Zondervan, 2015.

Spina, Frank Anthony. *The Faith of the Outsider: Exclusion and Inclusion in the Biblical Story*. Grand Rapids: Eerdmans, 2005.

Swamidass, S. Joshua. "Reframing Scopes." *Christianity Today*, May/Jun. 2025, 62–66.

Towner, W. Sibley. *Genesis*. Louisville: Westminster John Knox, 2001.

Treat, Jeremy R. *The Crucified King: Atonement and Kingdom in Biblical and Systematic Theology*. Grand Rapids: Zondervan, 2014.

Bibliography

Turner, Kenneth J. "Teaching Genesis 1 at a Christian College." In *Reading Genesis 1–2: An Evangelical Conversation*, edited by Daryl Charles, 187–205. Peabody, MA: Hendrickson, 2013.

Waltke, Bruce. *The Dance Between God and Humanity: Reading the Bible Today as the People of God*. Grand Rapids: Eerdmans, 2013.

———. *Genesis: A Commentary*. Grand Rapids: Zondervan, 2001.

Walton, John H. *Ancient Israelite Literature in Its Cultural Context: A Survey of Parallels Between Biblical and Ancient Near Eastern Texts*. Grand Rapids: Zondervan, 1989.

———. "Four Responses to Chapter Two." In *Reading Genesis 1–2: An Evangelical Conversation*, edited by Daryl Charles, 62–72. Peabody, MA: Hendrickson, 2013.

———. "Four Responses to Chapter Three." In *Reading Genesis 1–2: An Evangelical Conversation*, edited by Daryl Charles, 100–102. Peabody, MA: Hendrickson, 2013.

———. "Genesis and the Conceptual World of the Ancient Near East." In *The Cambridge Companion to Genesis*, edited by Bill T. Arnold, 148–67. Cambridge, UK: Cambridge University Press, 2022.

———. *The Lost World of Adam and Eve*. Downers Grove, IL: InterVarsity, 2015.

———. *The Lost World of Genesis One: Ancient Cosmology and the Origins Debate*. Downers Grove, IL: Intervarsity, 2009.

Wenham, Gordon J. *Genesis 1–15*. Waco, TX: Word, 1987.

———. "Genesis 1–11 As Protohistory." In *Genesis: History, Fiction, or Neither?: Three Views on the Bible's Earliest Chapters*, edited by Charles Halton and Stanley N. Gundry, 73–97. Grand Rapids: Zondervan, 2015.

Westermann, Claus. *Genesis: A Practical Commentary*. Grand Rapids: Eerdmans, 1987.

Wikipedia. "Pat Robertson." https://en.wikipedia.org/wiki/Pat_Robertson.

———. "Post-Election Lawsuits Related to the 2020 U.S. Presidential Election." https://en.wikipedia.org/wiki/Post-election_lawsuits_related_to_the_2020_U.S._presidential_election.

———. "Scopes Trial." Htpps://en.wikipedia.org/wiki/Scopes_trial.

Wright, N. T. *How God Became King: The Forgotten Story of The Gospels*. San Francisco: Harper One, 2011.

———. *Surprised by Scripture: Engaging Contemporary Issues*. San Francisco: Harper One, 2014.

www.ingramcontent.com/pod-product-compliance
Lightning Source LLC
Chambersburg PA
CBHW050811160426
43192CB00010B/1718